VEGETARIAN DISHES

Canadian Living's™

best

BY

Elizabeth Baird

AND

The Food Writers of Canadian Living Magazine
and The Canadian Living Test Kitchen

A MADISON PRESS BOOK

PRODUCED FOR

BALLANTINE BOOKS AND CANADIAN LIVING™

Ballantine Books
A Division of
Random House of
Canada Limited
1265 Aerowood Drive
Mississauga, Ontario
Canada
L4W 1B9

Canadian Living
Telemedia
Communications Inc.
25 Sheppard Avenue West
Suite 100
North York, Ontario
Canada
M2N 6S7

Canadian Cataloguing in Publication Data

Vegetarian dishes

(Canadian living's best)
Includes index.
ISBN 0-345-39843-2

1. Vegetarian cookery.
I. Title.   II. Series.

TX837.B34 1997   641.5'636   C97-930355-9

™Canadian Living is a trademark owned by
Telemedia Communications Inc. and licensed by The Madison Press Limited.
All trademark rights, registered and unregistered, are reserved worldwide.

EDITORIAL DIRECTOR: Hugh Brewster
SUPERVISING EDITOR: Wanda Nowakowska
PROJECT EDITOR: Beverley Sotolov
EDITORIAL ASSISTANCE: Beverley Renahan
PRODUCTION DIRECTOR: Susan Barrable
PRODUCTION COORDINATOR: Donna Chong
BOOK DESIGN AND LAYOUT: Gordon Sibley Design Inc.
COLOR SEPARATION: Colour Technologies
PRINTING AND BINDING: St. Joseph Printing Limited

CANADIAN LIVING ADVISORY BOARD: Elizabeth Baird, Bonnie Baker Cowan,
Anna Hobbs, Caren King

CANADIAN LIVING'S™ BEST VEGETARIAN DISHES
was produced by Madison Press Books,
which is under the direction of Albert E. Cummings

Madison Press Books
40 Madison Avenue
Toronto, Ontario, Canada
M5R 2S1

Printed in Canada

Contents

Introduction

Cooking vegetarian means opening the door to a whole world of delicious flavors, taste sensations and satisfaction. For someone unfamiliar with vegetarian food, this style of cooking may sound new and perhaps intimidating. But it's not all that novel. And it's certainly not intimidating.

Just think of the macaroni and cheese baking crusty and fragrant in the oven, or the corn chowder simmering on the stove, or the potato latkes and omelettes sizzling in the pan. All are examples of no-meat dishes whose aromas have welcomed hungry Canadian families home for generations.

Add to these favorites the pastas and pizzas, the frittatas and risottos, the stir-fries, lasagnas, quesadillas, hummus, paellas and curries, and you get a sample of the growing interest in, and acceptance of, ethnic cuisines at the Canadian table. These cuisines are a treasure trove of delicious vegetarian dishes, and as we take the cuisines into our lives, so we take the dishes into our hearts.

Vegetarian ingredients abound these days. They include the many different kinds of legumes — black beans, lentils and chick-peas, for example; the many grain products — couscous, barley, bagels, pasta or rolled oats; and, of course, the vegetables, with their medley of flavors and colors. All are the welcome components of a healthy diet. The good news is that not only are these ingredients available, they are also inexpensive items commonly stocked in the supermarket. Even tofu has gone mainstream and can be found nestled in with the herbs and greens of the produce department.

Please enjoy *Canadian Living's Best Vegetarian Dishes*. Its more than 100 recipes for main courses and appetizers will take the mystery out of vegetarian cooking with easy-to-cook dishes to tempt you for weeknight and entertaining eating.

Elizabeth Baird

Mexican Quesadilla Salad (p. 62)

Anytime Appetizers

Let the good times roll with appetizers that make parties more delicious and fun than ever before. These easy nibbles and noshes gather up all the best new flavors of quesadillas, bruschettas, phyllo tidbits and dips and please everyone on the guest list.

Roasted Mushroom and Pepper Phyllo Rounds ▶

A *first course for a sit-down dinner should be make-ahead and a delicious harbinger of the dishes to follow. Case in point — these crisp, golden pleated phyllo rounds, which hold a toss of roasted mushrooms, red peppers and Oka, one of Canada's finest cheeses.*

Per appetizer: about
- 245 calories
- 13 g fat
- good source of calcium
- 11 g protein
- 21 g carbohydrate

1 lb	small mushrooms	500 g
2 tbsp	red wine vinegar	25 mL
1/4 tsp	each salt and pepper	1 mL
1	jar (340 mL) roasted sweet red peppers	1
1 cup	fresh bread crumbs	250 mL
1 tbsp	liquid honey	15 mL
1/2 tsp	crushed dried mint	2 mL
10 oz	Oka or Port du Salut cheese	300 g
3 tbsp	sweet mustard	50 mL
12	sheets phyllo pastry	12
2 tbsp	butter, melted	25 mL
1	egg white, beaten	1

● Trim and quarter mushrooms; place on rimmed baking sheet. Sprinkle with vinegar and half each of the salt and pepper; toss to coat evenly. Bake in 400°F (200°C) oven, stirring occasionally, for 35 to 40 minutes or until tender and liquid is evaporated. Let cool slightly.

● Drain red peppers; pat dry with paper towels. Chop and place in large bowl. Add half of the bread crumbs, the honey, mint and remaining salt and pepper; toss to combine. Cut rind from cheese; shred and add to bowl along with mushrooms. Toss again; set aside. *(Filling can be covered and refrigerated for up to 1 day; stir before using.)*

● Blend mustard with 1 tbsp (15 mL) water; set aside. Layer 3 sheets of phyllo on work surface, keeping remaining phyllo covered with plastic wrap then damp towel, to prevent drying out. Using sharp knife and 8-inch (20 cm) round cake pan or cardboard template as guide, cut out 2 circles from each sheet, discarding trimmings.

● Place 2 circles side by side on work surface. Brush each lightly with mustard mixture. Top each with second circle; brush lightly with butter. Top each with remaining circles; brush again with mustard. Sprinkle 1 tbsp (15 mL) of the remaining bread crumbs in center of each circle. Top crumbs with heaping 1/2 cup (125 mL) of the filling.

● Fold one edge of phyllo to center over filling. Grasp point at edge of circle where first fold begins; fold point over filling into center, forming pleat. Continue folding phyllo over filling, overlapping pleats but leaving 1/2-inch (1 cm) diameter steam vent in center; press pleats to seal. Place on parchment paper-lined or greased baking sheet.

● Brush all over with egg white. Repeat to make 8 rounds. *(Rounds can be refrigerated for up to 12 hours. Or freeze, then wrap each in plastic wrap and store in airtight container for up to 2 weeks; increase baking time by 5 minutes.)* Bake in 400°F (200°C) oven for 20 minutes or until golden brown and crispy. Makes 8 appetizers.

Tex-Mex Appetizer Flan ▼

If party food is what you're doing up, and no-fuss preparation is what you're after, try making one large appetizer — this flan, for example — instead of a slew of nibbles.

Per piece: about
- 125 calories
- 7 g fat
- 3 g protein
- 13 g carbohydrate

1-1/2 cups	all-purpose flour	375 mL
1/2 cup	cornmeal	125 mL
2 tsp	chili powder	10 mL
1-1/2 tsp	ground cumin	7 mL
1/2 tsp	salt	2 mL
1/2 cup	butter, cubed	125 mL
1/4 cup	shortening, cubed	50 mL
1/3 cup	cold water	75 mL
	FILLING	
1	can (19 oz/540 mL) white kidney beans, drained and rinsed	1
1/2 cup	salsa	125 mL
1/4 cup	each chopped green onions and fresh coriander	50 mL
1/4 cup	sour cream	50 mL
2 tbsp	lemon juice	25 mL
Pinch	each salt and pepper	Pinch

	TOPPING	
1/2 cup	each chopped black olives, green onions and sweet red pepper	125 mL

● In bowl, stir together flour, cornmeal, chili powder, cumin and salt. With pastry blender or two knives, cut in butter and shortening until fine crumbs form. With fork, stir in water just until mixture clings together. Form into ball.

● Between sheets of waxed paper, roll out pastry and fit into 12- x 9-inch (30 x 23 cm) flan pan with removable bottom; trim edges. Prick bottom with fork. Line with parchment paper or foil and weigh down with pie weights or rice. Bake in 425°F (220°C) oven for 20 to 25 minutes or until golden brown around edges. Remove weights and paper. Bake for 10 minutes longer or until evenly golden. Let cool on rack. *(Pastry shell can be covered and set aside for up to 8 hours.)*

● FILLING: Meanwhile, in food processor, purée beans. Add salsa, green onions, coriander, sour cream, lemon juice, salt and pepper; pulse just until combined. *(Filling can be refrigerated in airtight container for up to 8 hours; let stand at room temperature for 30 minutes before proceeding.)* Spread filling in pastry shell.

● TOPPING: Combine, or individually arrange, olives, green onions and red pepper over flan. Cut into 24 pieces.

TIP: To make pastry cutouts, as in our photo, remove a little pastry before lining pan. Roll out and cut into shapes; bake on baking sheet in 425°F (220°C) oven for 8 to 10 minutes or until golden.

Caramelized Onion Quesadillas

1 tbsp	butter	15 mL
1 tbsp	vegetable oil	15 mL
3 cups	sliced onions (2 large)	750 mL
1 tsp	granulated sugar	5 mL
1 tsp	crumbled dried rosemary	5 mL
4 oz	Brie cheese, sliced, cream goat cheese (chèvre) or cream cheese	125 g
Pinch	each salt and pepper	Pinch
2	10-inch (25 cm) flour tortillas	2

● In large skillet, heat butter with oil over high heat; cook onions, sugar and rosemary, stirring occasionally, for 5 minutes. Reduce heat to medium-high; cook, stirring and scraping bottom of pan often, for 10 to 15 minutes or until onions are golden brown and very soft. Let cool to room temperature. *(Recipe can be prepared to this point and refrigerated in airtight container for up to 24 hours.)*

● In small bowl, stir together cheese, salt and pepper; evenly arrange over half of each tortilla. Evenly divide onions over cheese. Fold uncovered half over filling; press edges together. *(Quesadillas can be prepared to this point, covered and refrigerated for up to 3 hours.)* Bake on baking sheet in 425°F (220°C) oven, turning halfway through, for 10 minutes or until browned and crisp. Cut into wedges. Makes 4 servings.

Let the fun of a party or sit-down dinner begin with wedges of crisp, golden brown tortillas sandwiching melting gooey cheese and sweetly caramelized onions.

Per serving: about
- 290 calories
- 10 g protein
- 16 g fat
- 28 g carbohydrate

Green Onion Crêpes

1 tbsp	each sesame oil and canola oil	15 mL
12	green onions, diced	12
1 cup	all-purpose flour	250 mL
4	eggs, beaten	4
1 cup	beer or soda water (approx), at room temperature	250 mL
2 tbsp	each rice vinegar and soy sauce	25 mL
2	cloves garlic, minced	2
2	small dried hot red peppers, minced	2
1-1/2 tsp	salt	7 mL
	Coriander sprigs and green onions	

TIP: Serve crêpes with Firecracker Drizzle. To make; pour 3/4 cup (175 mL) fruit chutney, 1/4 cup (50 mL) medium or hot salsa and 1/2 cup (125 mL) water into a blender or food processor and blend until smooth. Serve hot or cold. Makes 1-1/2 cups (375 mL).

● In large skillet, heat sesame oil and canola oil over medium-high heat; stir-fry green onions for 30 seconds. Remove from heat.

● In bowl, mix together flour, eggs and beer; whisk in vinegar, soy sauce, garlic, hot red peppers and salt until fairly smooth. Add onions. Let rest for 15 minutes in refrigerator. (Batter should have consistency of thick cream; if too thick, add a little more beer.)

● Heat lightly greased or nonstick 6-inch (15 cm) crêpe pan over medium-high heat. Using 1/4 cup (50 mL) batter for each crêpe, pour into pan, swirling to coat evenly. Cook for about 30 seconds or until edge begins to brown; turn and cook for 30 seconds. Transfer crêpes to paper towel-lined tray; keep warm.

● To serve, fold crêpes into quarters; arrange on platter. Garnish with coriander and green onions. Makes 12 crêpes.

Edmonton writer and food editor Judy Schultz transformed the heavy green onion pancakes served in many Chinese restaurants into these delicate-textured crêpes that deliver a thump of onion, garlic and hot pepper flavor. Complement with your favorite Asian dipping sauce (see box).

Per crêpe: about
- 100 calories
- 4 g protein
- 4 g fat
- 11 g carbohydrate

TIP: For an easy appetizer, make small 3-inch (8 cm) round crêpes to wrap around tasty fillings.

TRENDY NEW TASTES IN MUSHROOMS

To feed our increasing taste for mushrooms, mushroom growers have brought new varieties of "exotic mushrooms" to market. Available now is the crimini, a woodsy brown version of the rounded white *agaracus*, the first commonly available mushroom. The crimini, allowed to grow as large as possible so that its top flattens to expose the gills, becomes the portobello. This giant is the darling of the stir-friers and barbecuers, who appreciate its intense flavor and firm texture. Also available is the shiitake. This mushroom is drier, making it a good keeper, and its taste is rich and deep. The beauty among the exotics is the oyster mushroom. Available in soft pinks, yellows, pearl and buff tones, it is more delicate in taste and requires more careful handling.

Summer Rolls with Lime Chili Dressing

This recipe was inspired by Eric Wah, chef and co-owner of the King and I restaurants in Edmonton and Calgary.

Per piece: about
• 60 calories   • 1 g protein
• 1 g fat   • 13 g carbohydrate

TIP: If rice paper wrappers are larger than 6 inches (15 cm), trim with sharp knife after soaking.

8 oz	shiitake mushrooms, stemmed	250 g
1 tbsp	vegetable oil	15 mL
1 tbsp	soy sauce	15 mL
1/2 tsp	granulated sugar	2 mL
1	English cucumber	1
1	large carrot	1
2	stalks celery	2
16	6-inch (15 cm) round rice paper wrappers	16
1 cup	loosely packed fresh coriander leaves	250 mL
	LIME CHILI DRESSING	
1/2 cup	granulated sugar	125 mL
1/4 cup	lime juice	50 mL
1/4 cup	white vinegar	50 mL
2 tbsp	soy sauce	25 mL
1	clove garlic, minced	1
1 tsp	Asian chili sauce	5 mL

● LIME CHILI DRESSING: In small saucepan, whisk together sugar, lime juice, vinegar, soy sauce, garlic, chili sauce and 1/4 cup (50 mL) water; cook over medium heat, stirring, for about 3 minutes or until sugar is dissolved. Let cool completely. (Dressing can be refrigerated in airtight container for up to 24 hours.)

● Cut mushrooms into 1/4-inch (5 mm) thick slices. In nonstick skillet, heat oil over medium-high heat; cook mushrooms, stirring often, for about 5 minutes or until browned and liquid is evaporated. Stir soy sauce with sugar; pour into pan and cook, stirring, until sauce is absorbed. Let cool completely.

● Core cucumber. Cut carrot, celery and cucumber lengthwise into scant 1/4-inch (5 mm) thick strips. Cut carrot and celery into 8-inch (20 cm) lengths; cut cucumber into 10-inch (25 cm) lengths. Drain any liquid from mushrooms. Immerse 1 rice paper wrapper in shallow pan of hot water until pliable, 5 to 7 seconds; place on work surface. Repeat soaking with 1 more rice paper; place on first, overlapping by three-quarters.

● Place about one-eighth of the mushrooms lengthwise along center of papers; stack with 1 piece each carrot and celery and 2 pieces cucumber, letting ends extend past paper. Sprinkle with 1 tbsp (15 mL) of the coriander.

● Starting at long side, roll up into cylinder, leaving ends open; cut in half crosswise. Place on tray; cover with damp cloth. Repeat with remaining ingredients. (Tray can be wrapped in plastic wrap and refrigerated for up to 1 hour.) Serve standing on cut end with dressing for dipping. Makes 16 pieces.

Chick-Pea Panisse

4 cups	milk	1 L
2 tbsp	butter	25 mL
2 cups	chick-pea flour	500 mL
1/2 tsp	salt	2 mL
Pinch	pepper	Pinch
3/4 cup	olive oil	175 mL

● In saucepan, bring milk and butter to boil over medium-high heat. Gradually whisk in flour; simmer, stirring constantly, for 5 minutes. Stir in salt and pepper. Pour into greased 9-inch (2.5 L) square cake pan. Refrigerate for 10 minutes. Cut into 3-inch (8 cm) long sticks, about 1/4 inch (5 mm) wide.

● In skillet, heat 1/4 cup (50 mL) of the oil over medium-high heat; sauté one-third of the sticks, turning once, for about 5 minutes or until golden on outside and soft inside. Repeat twice with remaining oil and sticks. Makes 78 sticks.

T*hese savory fried "sticks" will satisfy any hungry young crowd. For a smaller batch, halve all the ingredients except the pepper. Chick-pea flour, called besan, is available in Indian and Asian stores.*

Per stick: about
- 40 calories
- 3 g fat
- 1 g protein
- 2 g carbohydrate

Roasted Tomato Crostini ▼

1	French stick (baguette), 20 inches (50 cm) long	1
4 oz	soft goat cheese	125 g
20	fresh basil leaves	20
	ROASTED TOMATOES	
4 lb	ripe plum tomatoes (about 20 whole)	2 kg
4	cloves garlic, minced	4
1/4 cup	chopped fresh basil	50 mL
1/4 cup	olive oil	50 mL
1/4 tsp	each salt and pepper	1 mL

● ROASTED TOMATOES: Trim stem end of tomatoes; cut in half lengthwise. Arrange cut side up and without crowding on large foil-lined rimmed baking sheet.

● Stir together garlic, basil and oil; brush over tomatoes. Sprinkle with salt and pepper. Bake in 400°F (200°C) oven for 2 hours or until tomatoes are softened and shriveled and edges begin to darken. Let cool.

● Cut bread into 20 slices; place on baking sheet and broil until toasted.

● Evenly spread with goat cheese; top each with 2 tomato halves and 1 basil leaf. Makes 20 pieces.

S*et your tastebuds tingling with tongue-teasing roasted tomatoes atop grilled bread.*

Per piece: about
- 105 calories
- 5 g fat
- 3 g protein
- 13 g carbohydrate

Vineland Estates Bruschetta ▲

*M*aking and enjoying this
*lusty bruschetta from
Vineland Estates in the
Niagara Peninsula is the next
best thing to being there!*

Per piece: about
- 65 calories
- 2 g fat
- 2 g protein
- 9 g carbohydrate

1/4 cup	white wine vinegar	50 mL
2 tbsp	olive oil	25 mL
1 tbsp	chopped fresh parsley	15 mL
1 tsp	each granulated sugar and dried basil	5 mL
1/2 tsp	each dried thyme and dillweed	2 mL
1/4 tsp	each salt and pepper	1 mL
Dash	hot pepper sauce	Dash
Pinch	hot pepper flakes	Pinch
1	clove garlic, minced	1
2	tomatoes, chopped	2
1	cucumber, chopped	1
2	stalks celery, chopped	2
1	French stick (baguette), about 12 inches (30 cm) long	1
1/2 cup	shredded Asiago cheese	125 mL

● In bowl, whisk together vinegar, oil, parsley, sugar, basil, thyme, dillweed, salt, pepper, hot pepper sauce, hot pepper flakes and garlic. Add tomatoes, cucumber and celery; toss to combine. Set aside.

● Cut bread into twenty-four 1/2-inch (1 cm) thick slices; place on baking sheet and broil, turning once, until toasted.

● Spoon tomato mixture over toast; sprinkle with cheese. Broil for 1 minute. Makes 24 pieces.

Cheese Crackerbread

1/2 cup	warm water	125 mL
4	egg whites	4
1 tsp	salt	5 mL
1 tsp	granulated sugar	5 mL
1 tsp	active dry yeast	5 mL
2-1/2 cups	all-purpose flour (approx)	625 mL
1/3 cup	grated romano or Parmesan cheese	75 mL
1 tsp	dried thyme	5 mL
1 tbsp	each poppy seeds and sesame seeds	15 mL

● In bowl, combine water, egg whites, salt, sugar and yeast. With wooden spoon, stir in 2 cups (500 mL) of the flour, cheese and thyme; beat until smooth. Stir in enough of the remaining flour to form soft dough.

● Turn out dough onto lightly floured surface; knead several times to form ball. Place in greased bowl, turning to grease all over. Cover with plastic wrap; let rise for 45 minutes.

● Punch down dough; turn out onto lightly floured surface. Divide into 4 portions; roll out each into 1/8-inch (3 mm) thick circle or oval. Place on lightly greased baking sheet; prick all over with fork. Brush lightly with water; sprinkle with poppy seeds and sesame seeds.

● Bake in 400°F (200°C) oven for 10 to 15 minutes or until golden brown. Transfer to racks and let cool. Break into shards. *(Flatbread can be stored in airtight container for up to 3 days.)* Makes about 24 pieces.

Thin and crunchy, this flatbread is fabulous broken into shards and served as part of an appetizer tray.

Per piece: about
- 65 calories
- 1 g fat
- 3 g protein
- 10 g carbohydrate

Onion and Artichoke Focaccia

2 tbsp	olive oil	25 mL
5	onions, thinly sliced	5
1/2 tsp	dried thyme or herbes de Provence	2 mL
1/2 tsp	salt	2 mL
1/4 tsp	pepper	1 mL
1	jar (6 oz/170 mL) marinated artichoke hearts, drained and chopped	1
1/4 cup	coarsely chopped black olives	50 mL
1	baked flatbread or pizza crust (14 oz/400 g)	1
1/3 cup	shredded mozzarella cheese	75 mL
2 tbsp	freshly grated Parmesan cheese	25 mL

● In large skillet, heat oil over medium heat; cook onions, thyme, salt and pepper, stirring often, for about 20 minutes or until onions are very soft and caramelized. Remove from heat. Stir in artichokes and olives.

● Place flatbread on baking sheet; spread with onion mixture. Sprinkle with mozzarella and Parmesan cheeses. Bake in 375°F (190°C) oven for 12 to 15 minutes or until cheese is bubbly. Cut into 12 wedges. Makes 12 pieces.

Like pizza, focaccia lends itself to many toppings. Here's a trendy variation in which the mellow sweetness of the slowly caramelized onions is complemented by the tangy marinated artichoke hearts.

Per piece: about
- 160 calories
- 6 g fat
- 5 g protein
- 21 g carbohydrate

Pesto Focaccia with Tomatoes

Here's finger food in abundance. Serve hot or at room temperature to any hungry crowd.

Per piece: about
- 95 calories
- 3 g protein
- 3 g fat
- 13 g carbohydrate

1 tsp	granulated sugar	5 mL
1 cup	lukewarm water	250 mL
1	pkg traditional active dry yeast (or 1 tbsp/15 mL)	1
3-1/2 cups	all-purpose flour	875 mL
1 tsp	salt	5 mL
	ALL-SEASON PESTO	
2 cups	coarsely chopped fresh parsley	500 mL
1/4 cup	freshly grated Parmesan cheese	50 mL
2 tbsp	dried basil	25 mL
4	cloves garlic	4
1 tsp	salt	5 mL
1/4 tsp	pepper	1 mL
1/4 cup	extra-virgin olive oil	50 mL
	TOPPING	
12	cherry tomatoes, seeded and sliced	12
1/3 cup	pine nuts	75 mL
1 tbsp	freshly grated Parmesan cheese	15 mL
1/4 tsp	coarse salt (optional)	1 mL

● In large bowl, stir sugar into warm water until dissolved. Sprinkle in yeast; let stand for 10 minutes or until frothy.

● ALL-SEASON PESTO: Meanwhile, in food processor, finely chop together parsley, Parmesan cheese, basil, garlic, salt and pepper. With motor running, gradually pour in oil in thin steady stream until smooth. Reserve 1/4 cup (50 mL) for topping.

● Gradually whisk remaining pesto, 1 cup (250 mL) of the flour and salt into yeast mixture to make sticky dough. With wooden spoon, beat in 2-1/4 cups (550 mL) flour. Turn out dough onto lightly floured surface; knead, working in remaining flour, for 5 to 7 minutes or until dough is smooth and elastic.

● Place dough in greased bowl, turning to grease all over. Cover with plastic wrap; let rise until doubled in bulk, about 1 hour. Punch down dough; press onto greased 15- x 10-inch (40 x 25 cm) jelly roll pan.

● TOPPING: Spread reserved pesto over dough. Top with rows of tomatoes; sprinkle with nuts, gently pressing into dough. Sprinkle with Parmesan, and salt (if using).

● Bake in 425°F (220°C) oven for 25 minutes or until bottom is golden. Let cool on rack; cut into squares. *(Focaccia can be wrapped well and frozen in airtight container for up to 1 month; reheat in 350°F/180°C oven for 5 minutes.)* Makes 28 pieces.

PESTO POTATO PIZZA

You can also shape fiber-rich Bean Bread Dough (p. 15) into a pizza.

Prepare Bean Bread Dough to end of first rise. On lightly floured surface, roll out into 17- x 11-inch (43 x 28 cm) rectangle; place on lightly oiled baking sheet. Spread with 1/3 cup (75 mL) pesto, leaving 1/2-inch (1 cm) border (if pesto is very thick, stir in up to 1 tbsp/15 mL olive oil before spreading on dough). Thinly slice 4 cooked potatoes (peeled or unpeeled); place over pesto in single layer. Sprinkle with pepper. Top with 2 cups (500 mL) shredded Swiss cheese and 2 chopped tomatoes. Bake in lower third of 500°F (260°C) oven for about 15 minutes or until bottom is golden and crisp and cheese is melted. Makes 6 servings.

Per serving: about
- 620 calories • 25 g protein • 22 g fat • 83 g carbohydrate
- good source of fiber

Bean Bread Focaccia ▼

1 tbsp	cornmeal	15 mL
2 tbsp	extra-virgin olive oil	25 mL
1/4 tsp	each salt and pepper	1 mL
	BEAN BREAD DOUGH	
1 tbsp	granulated sugar	15 mL
1 cup	warm water	250 mL
2 tsp	active dry yeast	10 mL
1 cup	cooked or canned navy (white pea) beans, drained and rinsed	250 mL
2 tbsp	vegetable oil	25 mL
2-1/4 cups	all-purpose flour (approx)	550 mL
1 cup	whole wheat flour	250 mL
1-1/2 tsp	salt	7 mL

● BEAN BREAD DOUGH: In large bowl, stir sugar into water until dissolved. Sprinkle in yeast; let stand for 10 minutes or until frothy. Meanwhile, in food processor, purée beans with oil until smooth; add to yeast mixture. With wooden spoon, vigorously beat in 1 cup (250 mL) of the all-purpose flour, the whole wheat flour and salt; beat for about 1 minute or until sticky dough forms. Gradually stir in enough of the remaining flour to make stiff dough.

● Turn out dough onto lightly floured surface. Knead for about 8 minutes or until smooth, elastic and stiff, adding up to 1/4 cup (50 mL) more flour if necessary. Place in greased bowl, turning to grease all over. Cover with plastic wrap; let rise for 1 to 1-1/2 hours or until doubled in bulk.

● Cut dough into 4 portions; roll out each to 1/2-inch (1 cm) thick circle. Sprinkle cornmeal evenly over large rimmed baking sheet; place circles on top. Cover with towel; let rise for 30 minutes or until doubled in bulk.

● Brush circles with oil; press fingers into top to give dimpled effect. Sprinkle with salt and pepper. Bake in bottom third of 400°F (200°C) oven for about 20 minutes or until golden and bottoms sound hollow when tapped. Makes 4 servings.

*P*uréed beans enrich a yeast dough that's versatile enough to triple as bread, a pizza base (see p. 14) or individual focaccias.

Per serving: about
- 570 calories
- 15 g fat
- very high source of fibre
- 16 g protein
- 93 carbohydrate
- excellent source of iron

Roasted Garlic and Eggplant Dip ▲

Roasting fortifies the mild flavor of eggplant and takes the bite out of garlic, enabling these ingredients to blend into a mellow, creamy, smooth dip that goes best with bread and crisp crackers. Try it on Cheese Crackerbread (p. 13), toasted or fresh pitas, melba toasts and lavosh.

Per tbsp (15 mL): about
- 15 calories
- trace fat
- 1 g protein
- 2 g carbohydrate

2	eggplants (about 2 lb/1 kg total)	2
6	cloves garlic (unpeeled)	6
1/2 cup	light sour cream	125 mL
1 tbsp	each chopped fresh coriander and basil (or 1 tsp/5 mL each dried)	15 mL
1 tbsp	Dijon mustard	15 mL
2 tsp	balsamic or red wine vinegar	10 mL
1/4 tsp	each salt and pepper	1 mL

● With fork, prick eggplants all over; place on lightly greased baking sheet. Bake in 375°F (190°C) oven for 35 minutes. Add garlic to sheet. Bake for about 25 minutes or until eggplants are very tender and garlic is tender. Let stand until cool enough to handle.

● Cut eggplant in half lengthwise; with spoon, scoop flesh into food processor. Squeeze garlic onto eggplant. Add sour cream; purée until smooth. Scrape into small serving bowl.

● Stir in coriander, basil, mustard, vinegar, salt and pepper. Cover and refrigerate for at least 1 hour or for up to 4 hours. Makes about 2 cups (500 mL).

Spinach and Cumin Dip

1	pkg (10 oz/284 g) fresh spinach, trimmed	1
3	green onions, chopped	3
1/2 cup	light sour cream	125 mL
4 oz	light cream cheese, softened	125 g
1 tbsp	lemon juice	15 mL
1/4 tsp	each ground cumin, coriander and salt	1 mL

● Rinse spinach; shake off excess water. In large saucepan, cook spinach over medium heat, covered and with just the water clinging to leaves, for about 2 minutes or until wilted. Drain well in colander, squeezing out moisture; transfer to food processor.

● Add onions, sour cream, cream cheese, lemon juice, cumin, coriander and salt; purée until smooth. Spoon into small serving bowl. *(Dip can be covered and refrigerated for up to 1 day.)* Makes 1-1/3 cups (325 mL).

*H*ere's a lightened-up spinach dip with low-key seasonings that will please all tastebuds. Spoon leftovers onto baked potatoes or over a bowl of plain pasta.

Per tbsp (15 mL): about
- 25 calories
- 1 g protein
- 2 g fat
- 2 g carbohydrate

Fresh Beet and Onion Dip

1/2 cup	quark cheese, light sour cream or light cream cheese	125 mL
1/2 cup	2% plain yogurt	125 mL
1/4 cup	shredded raw beet	50 mL
2	green onions, finely chopped	2
2 tsp	lemon juice	10 mL
1/4 tsp	each salt, pepper and granulated sugar	1 ml

● In small serving bowl, stir together quark, yogurt, beet, onions, lemon juice, salt, pepper and sugar. *(Dip can be covered and refrigerated for up to 8 hours.)* Makes 1-1/4 cups (300 mL).

*A*uthor Anne Lindsay created this striking pink dip that uses grated raw beets — an uncommon vegetable in appetizers.

Per tbsp (15 mL): about
- 11 calories
- 1 g protein
- 1 g fat
- 1 g carbohydrate

Creamy Fresh Herb Dip with Veggies

1	bunch broccoli	1
3	stalks celery	3
3	carrots	3
2	sweet red peppers	2
1	cucumber	1
	HERB DIP	
1 cup	2% plain yogurt	250 mL
1 cup	light sour cream	250 mL
1	clove garlic, minced	1
3 tbsp	chopped fresh parsley	50 mL
2 tbsp	each chopped fresh chives and thyme (or 2 tsp/10 mL dried)	25 mL

1 tbsp	Dijon mustard	15 mL
1/4 tsp	each salt and pepper	1 mL
1 tbsp	lemon juice	15 mL

● Cut broccoli into bite-size florets; reserve stalks for another use. Cut celery, carrots, red peppers and cucumber into sticks.

● HERB DIP: In small serving bowl, stir together yogurt, sour cream, garlic, parsley, chives, thyme, mustard, salt and pepper. *(Dip can be covered and refrigerated for up to 24 hours.)* Just before serving, stir in lemon juice. Serve with vegetables. Makes 8 servings.

*E*veryone needs an easy dip for family picnics and parties, and this one is ideal. You can also serve it with fresh seasonal vegetables, in place of a side salad at a meal, or as a healthy way to satisfy those afternoon and evening snack attacks.

Per tbsp (15 mL): about
- 105 calories
- 6 g protein
- 3 g fat
- 16 g carbohydrate
- good source of calcium

Tzatziki

This thickened yogurt-and-cucumber combo is wonderfully versatile. Serve it as a simple dip for pita, dollop it on baked white or sweet potatoes, spread it over tortillas before you top with beans or slather it over a tasty vegetarian patty.

Per tbsp (15 mL): about
- 20 calories
- 1 g protein
- 1 g fat
- 2 g carbohydrate

1-1/3 cups	plain yogurt	325 mL
One-third	English cucumber	One-third
1/2 tsp	salt	2 mL
2 tsp	each olive oil and lemon juice	10 mL
1	clove garlic, minced	1
1/4 tsp	pepper	1 mL

● Line sieve with double thickness cheesecloth; set over bowl. Add yogurt; drain in refrigerator for at least 3 hours or for up to 24 hours or until reduced to about 1 cup (250 mL).

● Meanwhile, peel and grate cucumber into another sieve; sprinkle with half of the salt. Let drain for 1 hour.

● In small serving bowl, stir together yogurt, cucumber, remaining salt, oil, lemon juice, garlic and pepper. Makes 1 cup (250 mL).

Tortellini with Feta Dip

Tortellini are the ideal toothpick appetizer to serve with this zesty feta dip, but water crackers, sliced baguette or any of the popular vegetable dippers are equally delicious.

Per appetizer: about
- 220 calories
- 9 g protein
- 11 g fat
- 21 g carbohydrate

1/2 cup	crumbled feta cheese	125 mL
2 tbsp	lemon juice	25 mL
2 tbsp	olive oil	25 mL
2 tbsp	water	25 mL
1/4 tsp	dried oregano	1 mL
1/4 tsp	ground cumin	1 mL
2 tbsp	minced onion	25 mL
1	clove garlic, minced	1
	Chopped fresh parsley	
1	pkg (255 g) vegetable- or cheese-filled tortellini	1

● In food processor, purée together cheese, lemon juice, oil, water, oregano and cumin until smooth. Stir in onion and garlic. Spoon into small serving bowl; garnish with parsley. *(Dip can be covered and refrigerated for up to 2 hours.)* Place dip on platter.

● In saucepan of boiling salted water, cook tortellini according to package directions or just until tender. Drain well and rinse with cold water. Arrange around dip. Makes 6 appetizers.

Black Bean Tapenade

Thick and chunky, this bean spread flavored with Provençal black olives, capers and garlic is a natural on toasted baguette or tucked into pita with lettuce, sprouts and tomatoes.

Per tbsp (15 mL): about
- 20 calories
- 1 g protein
- trace fat
- 3 g carbohydrate

1	can (19 oz/540 mL) black beans, drained and rinsed	1
1/4 cup	black olives, pitted	50 mL
1	clove garlic, minced	1
2 tbsp	lemon juice	25 mL
1 tbsp	capers, drained	15 mL
1 tbsp	olive oil	15 mL
1 tsp	dried thyme	5 mL
1 tsp	Dijon mustard	5 mL

● In food processor, combine black beans, olives, garlic, lemon juice, capers, oil, thyme and mustard; purée until smooth. Spoon into small serving bowl. *(Tapenade can be covered and refrigerated for up to 8 hours.)* Makes 2 cups (500 mL).

Hummus with Sun-Dried Tomatoes ▲

1	can (19 oz/540 mL) chick-peas, drained and rinsed	1
1/4 cup	drained oil-packed sun-dried tomatoes	50 mL
1/4 cup	water	50 mL
3 tbsp	lemon juice	50 mL
2 tbsp	olive oil	25 mL
1 tsp	ground cumin	5 mL
1/2 tsp	salt	2 mL
1/2 tsp	hot pepper sauce	2 mL
2	cloves garlic, minced	2

● In food processor, purée chick-peas until coarse. Add tomatoes, water, lemon juice, oil, cumin, salt and hot pepper sauce; process until smooth. Stir in garlic. Spoon into small serving bowl. *(Hummus can be covered and refrigerated for up to 24 hours.)* Makes about 1-1/2 cups (375 mL).

T*his inspired update on a Greek classic might as easily be called "Pantry Hummus," since all the ingredients can be stored and waiting in the cupboard whenever you need a wonderful last-minute dip.*

Per tbsp (15 mL): about
- 35 calories
- 1 g protein
- 2 g fat
- 4 g carbohydrate

TIP: For a change of taste, replace the sun-dried tomatoes with roasted red peppers.

Casseroles and Savory Pies

Hot out of the oven come crusty gratins, golden pastry-topped vegetable medleys, new impressive lasagnas, rice and pasta bakes — inspiration for potlucks and buffets, and ideal candidates for a comfy "Just add a salad and crusty bread" kind of menu.

Asparagus Gratin ▶

Asparagus finds its soul mate in mushrooms. Here, the two pair up in a brunch or supper dish that has echoes of quiche but is much lower in fat.

Per serving: about
- 160 calories
- 11 g protein
- 8 g fat
- 13 g carbohydrate
- good source of calcium

2 tsp	butter	10 mL
2	onions, chopped	2
6 cups	thickly sliced mushrooms (1 lb/500 g)	1.5 L
1/3 cup	all-purpose flour	75 mL
1 lb	asparagus	500 g
3	eggs	3
1-1/2 cups	1% milk	375 mL
1 tsp	Dijon mustard	5 mL
1/2 tsp	salt	2 mL
Pinch	each cayenne pepper and grated nutmeg	Pinch
1 cup	shredded Swiss cheese	250 mL

● In nonstick skillet, melt butter over medium-high heat; cook onions, stirring occasionally, for 5 minutes. Add mushrooms; cook, stirring often, for about 8 minutes or until lightly browned. Sprinkle with flour; cook, stirring, for 1 minute. Remove from heat.

● Meanwhile, snap ends off asparagus; cut into 1-inch (2.5 cm) pieces. In saucepan of boiling salted water, cook asparagus for about 3 minutes or until tender-crisp. Drain and refresh under cold water; drain again. Set aside.

● In large bowl, beat eggs lightly; whisk in milk, mustard, salt, cayenne and nutmeg; add onion mixture, asparagus and half of the Swiss cheese.

● Pour into greased 11- x 7-inch (2 L) baking dish, smoothing top. Sprinkle with remaining cheese. Bake in 350°F (180°C) oven for 50 to 60 minutes or just until set. Broil for 2 minutes. Makes 8 servings.

FRESH ASPARAGUS

Asparagus — the fresher the better! Choose straight firm green asparagus (thin stalks for salads and thick for best flavor as a side dish) with tightly closed purple-tinged tips. To store, remove elastic bands or twist ties; wrap in towels and enclose in plastic bag. Refrigerate for up to 2 days. One pound (500 g) serves two generously and yields about 3 cups (750 mL) chopped.

Squash and Mushroom Gratin

Easy to make, and just right served with a big salad and crusty bread, this layered dish is impressive enough for weekend entertaining.

Per serving: about
- 160 calories
- 9 g protein
- 10 g fat
- 11 g carbohydrate
- excellent source of calcium

3 cups	sliced mushrooms (8 oz/250 g)	750 mL
1	onion, thinly sliced	1
2	cloves garlic, minced	2
1 tsp	dried marjoram	5 mL
1 tsp	salt	5 mL
1/2 tsp	pepper	2 mL
Half	butternut squash (1 lb/500 g)	Half
2 tsp	each cornstarch and vegetable oil	10 mL
1-1/2 cups	shredded Swiss cheese	375 mL

● In bowl, toss together mushrooms, onion, garlic, marjoram, half of the salt and the pepper. Peel and seed squash; slice thinly. In separate bowl, toss squash with cornstarch, oil and remaining salt.

● Spread half of the mushroom mixture in 11- x 7-inch (2 L) glass baking dish; top with half each of the squash mixture and cheese. Repeat layers. Bake in 400°F (200°C) oven for about 40 minutes or until squash is tender. Let stand for 10 minutes. Makes 4 servings.

Garden-Fresh Gratin

Summer is the perfect time to try out this light dish chock-full of ripe tomatoes, red and yellow peppers and fresh thyme.

Per serving: about
- 240 calories
- 16 g protein
- 11 g fat
- 22 g carbohydrate
- high source of fiber
- excellent source of calcium

1	eggplant (about 1 lb/500 g)	1
1	each sweet red and yellow pepper	1
2	tomatoes	2
1	small onion, sliced	1
2	cloves garlic, minced	2
2 tsp	chopped fresh thyme (or 1/2 tsp/2 mL dried)	10 mL
1 cup	shredded light Swiss-style cheese	250 mL
1/2 cup	shredded part-skim mozzarella cheese	125 mL
3/4 tsp	salt	4 mL
1/2 tsp	pepper	2 mL
1 cup	fresh bread crumbs	250 mL
1 tbsp	butter	15 mL

● Trim eggplant; cut crosswise into 1/4-inch (5 mm) thick slices. Core and seed red and yellow peppers; cut into rings. Slice tomatoes thinly. Set vegetables aside.

● In bowl, toss together onion, garlic and thyme. In separate bowl, toss together Swiss and mozzarella cheeses.

● Arrange half of the eggplant, overlapping slightly, in lightly greased 8-inch (2 L) square baking dish. Sprinkle with half each of the salt and pepper. Top with red pepper and half each of the onion mixture, tomatoes and cheese. Repeat layers once, using yellow pepper. Sprinkle with bread crumbs; dot with butter.

● Bake in 400°F (200°C) oven for 45 to 55 minutes or until golden and vegetables are softened. Let stand for 10 minutes before serving. Makes 4 servings.

Barley and Corn Casserole ▲

1 tbsp	vegetable oil	15 mL
1	onion, chopped	1
3	cloves garlic, minced	3
2	carrots, finely chopped	2
1 cup	pearl or pot barley	250 mL
3 cups	vegetable stock	750 mL
2 cups	corn kernels	500 mL
1/2 cup	chopped fresh parsley	125 mL
Pinch	each salt and pepper	Pinch

● In heavy flameproof casserole, heat oil over medium-high heat; cook onion, garlic and carrots, stirring often, for 4 minutes or until onion is softened.

● Stir in barley; pour in stock. Cover and bake in 350°F (180°C) oven for 1 hour.

● Stir in corn, parsley, salt and pepper. Bake for 5 minutes or until corn is heated through and barley is tender. *(Casserole can be cooled in refrigerator, covered and stored for up to 2 days. To reheat, stir in 1/2 cup/ 125 mL stock or water; bake until heated through.)* Makes 8 servings.

Corn adds vivid color and a satisfying crunchy texture to baked barley. Note that pot and pearl barley are interchangeable in this recipe, and in most others. Pearl barley has more of its outer coat polished off than pot barley, hence its pearly name and color.

Per serving: about
- 155 calories
- 4 g protein
- 2 g fat
- 32 g carbohydrate
- very high source of fiber

Potato Carrot Kugel ▲

*F*rugal and heartwarming, this traditional casserole is ideal for suppers on brisk fall days or when winter howls at the kitchen door.

Per serving: about
- 415 calories
- 20 g fat
- high source of fiber
- 16 g protein
- 43 g carbohydrate
- good source of calcium and iron

2 tbsp	vegetable oil	25 mL
1	onion, thinly sliced	1
3 cups	sliced mushrooms (8 oz/250 g)	750 mL
1-1/2 tsp	dried thyme	7 mL
4	baking potatoes (about 2 lb/1 kg)	4
2	large carrots	2
3	eggs	3
3/4 tsp	salt	4 mL
1/2 tsp	pepper	2 mL
1 cup	shredded Cheddar cheese	250 mL

● In large skillet, heat oil over medium heat; cook onion, mushrooms and thyme, stirring occasionally, for about 10 minutes or until softened. Place in large bowl.

● Peel and grate potatoes and carrots; add to onion mixture and toss to mix well. Whisk together eggs, salt and pepper; add to potato mixture. Add cheese and toss to mix well.

● Spoon into greased 11- x 7-inch (2 L) baking dish; bake in top third of 400°F (200°C) oven for 1 hour or until golden and crispy. Makes 4 main-course servings.

Veggie, Pasta and Bean Bake

2 tbsp	butter	25 mL
3	cloves garlic, minced	3
2	onions, chopped	2
2	carrots, diced	2
1 tbsp	red wine vinegar	15 mL
1/2 tsp	crushed dried rosemary	2 mL
1/2 tsp	pepper	2 mL
Pinch	hot pepper flakes	Pinch
3 cups	spaghetti sauce	750 mL
1	can (19 oz/540 mL) romano or red kidney beans, drained and rinsed	1
2 cups	rotini pasta	500 mL
2 cups	chopped broccoli	500 mL
1/3 cup	freshly grated Romano cheese	75 mL

● In nonstick skillet, melt butter over medium-low heat; cover and cook garlic, onions and carrots, stirring occasionally, for about 10 minutes or until softened.

● Stir in vinegar, rosemary, pepper and hot pepper flakes; cook, covered, for about 15 minutes or until onions are very soft. Stir in spaghetti sauce and bring to boil; reduce heat and simmer for about 5 minutes or until thickened. Stir in beans.

● Meanwhile, in large pot of boiling salted water, cook pasta for 5 minutes. Add broccoli; cook for about 1 minute or until pasta is almost tender and broccoli is bright green and still crisp. Drain and return to pot. Stir in tomato sauce.

● Pour into greased 8-inch (2 L) square baking dish; sprinkle with Romano cheese. Cover with foil. *(Casserole can be prepared to this point, cooled in refrigerator and stored for up to 4 hours. Let stand at room temperature for 30 minutes. Add 30 minutes to baking time.)* Bake in 350°F (180°C) oven for about 35 minutes or until hot throughout. Broil, uncovered, for about 2 minutes or until browned and bubbling. Makes 4 servings.

Tired of plain pasta and tomato sauce? Liven up uninspired menus with this hearty rotini-and-kidney-bean casserole that's not only tasty but also rich in fiber, calcium and iron.

Per serving: about
- 540 calories
- 15 g fat
- very high source of fiber
- excellent source of iron
- 21 g protein
- 85 g carbohydrate
- good source of calcium

BEAN BASICS

Canned Beans

● Many varieties of canned beans are available: red kidney; white pea (navy); romano; white kidney; black; chick-peas (garbanzo beans); pigeon peas. Each variety has a slightly different flavor, texture, shape and color. Use mixtures to make your favorite recipe more interesting.

● A 19-oz (540 mL) can of beans, drained, yields about 2 cups (500 mL).

● Drain and rinse canned beans before using to reduce saltiness, sliminess and the gas-producing element contained in the liquid.

● Introduce beans to your diet slowly to let your digestive system adjust to the different sugars.

Dried Beans

● One cup (250 mL) dried beans yields about 2 cups (500 mL) cooked.

● To cook dried beans, rinse and soak for 12 hours in 3 times their volume of cold water. (Or, for a quick soak, bring to boil and boil gently for 2 minutes. Remove from heat, cover and let stand for 1 hour.) Drain off water; rinse. In saucepan, cover beans with 3 times their volume of water and bring to a boil. Reduce

heat and simmer, covered, for 1 to 2 hours (depending on the variety) or until tender.

● Discarding soaking and cooking liquids and rinsing with fresh water decreases the amount of gas-producing sugars in the dish.

Frozen Beans

● For a change, look in the freezer section for increasingly available mixtures of frozen beans.

Raclette Casserole

A Swiss dish, raclette is simply cheese melted by the fire, then usually scraped onto potatoes. Swiss-type cheeses, such as Emmenthal, can be substituted for Oka cheese in this delicious casserole version.

Per serving: about
- 620 calories
- 35 g fat
- high source of fiber
- good source of iron
- 37 g protein
- 40 g carbohydrate
- excellent source of calcium

6	large new potatoes (about 2-1/2 lb/1.25 kg)	6
1	large carrot, sliced	1
1	large stalk broccoli	1
2 tbsp	butter	25 mL
3 cups	sliced mushrooms (about 8 oz/250 g)	750 mL
	Salt and pepper	
6 cups	shredded Oka cheese (about 1-1/2 lb/750 g)	1.5 L

● Peel potatoes if desired. In large saucepan of boiling salted water, cook potatoes for 20 to 30 minutes or just until tender. Add carrot during last 5 minutes of cooking time. With slotted spoon, remove potatoes and carrot; let cool slightly. Slice potatoes thinly; set aside. Set carrots aside separately.

● Peel broccoli stalk; cut stalk and florets into bite-size pieces. Add to saucepan; cook for 2 minutes. Drain and refresh under cold water; set aside. In skillet, melt butter over medium heat; cook mushrooms, stirring occasionally, for 6 minutes or until tender.

● In shallow greased 8-cup (2 L) baking dish, overlap half of the potatoes. Season with salt and pepper to taste. Sprinkle with 2 cups (500 mL) of the cheese. Layer carrot, broccoli and mushrooms on top. Season with salt and pepper to taste. Sprinkle with 1 cup (250 mL) of the cheese.

● Top with overlapping slices of remaining potatoes. Season with salt and pepper to taste. Sprinkle with remaining cheese. *(Can be covered and refrigerated for up to 2 hours.)* Bake in 350°F (180°C) oven for 30 to 40 minutes or until heated through and cheese is melted. Broil for 1 to 2 minutes or until top is browned. Makes about 6 servings.

Spinach Pie

A 10-ounce (284 gram) bag of fresh spinach, trimmed, washed and cooked just until wilted, can replace the frozen in this pie. A dollop of light sour cream would add a nice finishing touch.

Per serving: about
- 470 calories
- 29 g fat
- excellent source of calcium
- 17 g protein
- 35 g carbohydrate
- good source of iron

	Pastry for 9-inch (23 cm) double-crust pie	
2 tsp	Dijon mustard	10 mL
1	egg yolk	1
1 tbsp	milk	15 mL
	FILLING	
1 tbsp	vegetable oil	15 mL
1	large onion, chopped	1
2	cloves garlic, minced	2
2 cups	sliced mushrooms (about 6 oz/175 g)	500 mL
1	pkg (300 g) frozen spinach, thawed and squeezed dry	1
1 tbsp	chopped fresh oregano	15 mL
1 tsp	salt	5 mL
Pinch	pepper	Pinch
1 cup	part-skim ricotta cheese	250 mL
1 cup	fresh bread crumbs	250 mL
2	eggs, lightly beaten	2
1/2 cup	freshly grated Parmesan cheese	125 mL

● FILLING: In large nonstick skillet, heat oil over medium heat; cook onion, garlic and mushrooms, stirring occasionally, for about 7 minutes or until onion is softened. Stir in spinach, oregano, salt and pepper. Mix together ricotta cheese, bread crumbs, eggs and Parmesan cheese; stir into spinach mixture. Set aside.

● On lightly floured surface, roll out half of the pastry and fit into 9-inch (23 cm) quiche dish. Brush bottom with mustard. Spoon in filling. Roll out remaining pastry and fit over filling; trim and crimp edge.

● Mix egg yolk with milk; brush over pastry. Cut steam vents in top. Bake in 375°F (190°C) oven for 35 to 40 minutes or until golden brown. Makes 6 servings.

Deep-Dish Sweet Potato Pot Pie

2 tbsp	olive oil	25 mL
3	cloves garlic, minced	3
1	onion, chopped	1
1 tbsp	paprika	15 mL
2 tsp	ground cumin	10 mL
1/2 tsp	each salt and pepper	2 mL
1/4 tsp	cinnamon	1 mL
1/4 cup	all-purpose flour	50 mL
3/4 cup	vegetable stock or water	175 mL
1	can (28 oz/796 mL) tomatoes	1
4	sweet potatoes, peeled and cubed (about 2 lb/1 kg)	4
12 oz	green beans	375 g
1	can (19 oz/540 mL) chick-peas, drained and rinsed	1
	PASTRY	
1-1/2 cups	all-purpose flour	375 mL
1 tsp	paprika	5 mL
1/2 tsp	each ground cumin and salt	2 mL
1/4 tsp	cayenne pepper	1 mL
1/4 cup	each butter and shortening, cubed	50 mL
1	egg yolk	1
1 tsp	vinegar	5 mL
	Ice water	

● PASTRY: In bowl, stir together flour, paprika, cumin, salt and cayenne. With pastry blender or two knives, cut in butter and shortening until in fine crumbs with a few larger pieces. In measuring cup and using fork, beat egg yolk with vinegar; add enough ice water to make 1/3 cup (75 mL). Pour over flour mixture all at once; stir with fork just until dough starts to clump together. Press into disc; wrap and refrigerate for 30 minutes. *(Pastry can be refrigerated for up to 3 days or frozen for up to 2 weeks; let thawed or cold dough stand at room temperature for 15 minutes.)*

● In large saucepan, heat oil over medium heat; cook garlic, onion, paprika, cumin, salt, pepper and cinnamon, stirring often, for 5 minutes or until onion is softened. Sprinkle with flour; cook, stirring, for 1 minute. Whisk in stock; add tomatoes, breaking up with spoon. Add sweet potatoes; bring to boil. Reduce heat, cover and simmer, stirring occasionally, for 15 minutes or until sweet potatoes are almost tender.

● Trim and cut green beans into 1-inch (2.5 cm) pieces. Add to pot along with chick-peas; simmer, covered, for 10 minutes. Uncover and simmer for 5 minutes or until thickened slightly, potatoes are tender and beans are tender-crisp. *(Filling can be cooled in refrigerator and stored in airtight container for up to 2 days; let stand at room temperature for 1 hour before continuing.)*

● Transfer filling to shallow 10-cup (2.5 L) casserole. On lightly floured surface, roll out pastry to fit dish, leaving 1-inch (2.5 cm) overhang. Place over filling; fold overhang under to rest just over edge of dish; crimp pastry. With 2-inch (5 cm) round cookie cutter, cut out steam vent in center; with knife, cut attractive steam vents around center. Bake in 400°F (200°C) oven for about 30 minutes or until pastry is golden and filling is bubbling. Makes 6 servings.

I*f a festive vegetarian alternative to turkey is what you're looking for at Thanksgiving or Christmas, this flavorful and satisfying dish is sure to tempt everyone at the table — including those partial to the holiday bird! In fact, it's special enough to serve at any entertaining occasion.*

Per serving: about
- 615 calories
- 24 g fat
- very high source of fiber
- 14 g protein
- 88 g carbohydrate
- excellent source of iron

TIPS

● If preparing filling ahead of time, add up to 1/4 cup (50 mL) tomato juice before baking.

● A square 10- or 9-inch (25 or 23 cm) casserole dish is ideal.

Hearty Vegetable Pot Pie ▶

When it comes time to tote a casserole to a potluck or you need to get a head start on entertaining, don't forget this colorful medley of winter vegetables baked under a savory golden crust.

Per serving: about
- 450 calories
- 21 g fat
- very high source of fiber
- 10 g protein
- 57 g carbohydrate
- good source of iron

TIP: When preparing the pot pie, be sure not to overcook the vegetables initially, because they will cook further while baking.

2 tbsp	butter	25 mL
4 cups	sliced carrots (2 lb/1 kg)	1 L
3 cups	sliced parsnips (1 lb/500 g)	750 mL
3 cups	sliced mushrooms (8 oz/250 g)	750 mL
2	onions, chopped	2
2	cloves garlic, minced	2
1 tsp	dried tarragon	5 mL
1/2 tsp	each salt and pepper	2 mL
2 cups	frozen peas	500 mL
1	can (19 oz/540 mL) corn kernels, drained (or 2 cups/500 mL frozen)	1
3 tbsp	all-purpose flour	50 mL
	SAUCE	
3 tbsp	butter	50 mL
1/2 cup	all-purpose flour	125 mL
2 cups	hot milk	500 mL
1 cup	vegetable stock	250 mL
2 tbsp	Dijon mustard	25 mL
1-1/2 tsp	grated lemon rind	7 mL
Pinch	each salt and pepper	Pinch
	PASTRY	
2 cups	all-purpose flour	500 mL
1/2 tsp	each salt and dried tarragon	2 mL
Pinch	pepper	Pinch
1/3 cup	each butter and shortening, cubed	75 mL
1	egg	1
1 tsp	vinegar	5 mL
	Ice water	
1 tbsp	milk	15 mL

● PASTRY: In bowl, stir together flour, salt, tarragon and pepper. Using pastry blender or two knives, cut in butter and shortening until in fine crumbs with a few larger pieces. In measuring cup and using fork, beat egg with vinegar; add enough ice water to make 1/2 cup (125 mL). Pour over flour mixture all at once; stir with fork just until dough holds together. Press into disc; wrap and refrigerate for 30 minutes.

● Meanwhile, in large shallow Dutch oven, melt butter over medium heat. Add carrots, parsnips, mushrooms, onions, garlic, tarragon, salt and pepper; cover and cook for about 12 minutes or just until carrots begin to soften. Uncover and cook, stirring, for 3 to 5 minutes or until moisture is evaporated. Transfer to large bowl; let cool.

● SAUCE: In same pan, melt butter over medium heat; stir in flour and cook, stirring, for 1 minute, without browning. Gradually whisk in milk and vegetable stock; bring to boil, whisking constantly. Reduce heat to medium-low; cook, whisking often, for about 15 minutes or until thickened to consistency of pudding. Whisk in mustard, lemon rind, salt and pepper. Place plastic wrap or waxed paper directly on surface; let cool.

● Add peas, corn and flour to vegetable mixture in bowl, stirring gently to mix. Pour cooled sauce over top, stirring to coat. Pour into 10-cup (2.5 L) oval or 13- x 9-inch (3 L) glass baking dish. Set aside.

● On lightly floured surface, roll out chilled pastry to 1/4-inch (5 mm) thick oval or rectangle. Place over vegetable mixture, trimming to leave 1-inch (2.5 cm) overhang. Reserve scraps. Pinch edges of pastry over rim of dish to seal and flute.

● Reroll reserved scraps. Using 1 1/2 inch (4 cm) star-shaped cookie cutter, cut out shapes. Arrange on waxed paper-lined baking sheet.

● Brush cutouts and pastry top with milk. Cut three 1-1/2-inch (4 cm) stars out of pastry top; brush stars with milk. Slash steam vents in remaining top. Arrange cutouts decoratively over top.

● Bake in 400°F (200°C) oven for 50 to 60 minutes or until pastry is golden and filling is bubbling. Let stand for 15 minutes before serving. Makes 10 servings.

Mediterranean Vegetable Pie

Roasted vegetables and roasted garlic are highlights of a wonderfully rustic pie. Enjoy a wedge with a toss of greens and late-afternoon sunshine.

Per serving: about
- 490 calories
- 30 g fat
- high source of fiber
- 13 g protein
- 45 g carbohydrate
- good source of calcium and iron

TIP: Instead of roasting your own, you can use 1 jar (340 mL) roasted red peppers, drained.

1-3/4 cups	all-purpose flour	425 mL
1 tsp	salt	5 mL
1 tsp	baking powder	5 mL
1/3 cup	olive oil	75 mL
1/3 cup	milk	75 mL
2	eggs	2
	FILLING	
1/4 cup	olive oil	50 mL
2	zucchini	2
2	onions	2
1	eggplant	1
1 tsp	salt	5 mL
1	head garlic	1
3	roasted red peppers, peeled and sliced	3
1 cup	shredded fontina or mozzarella cheese	250 mL
1/4 cup	chopped fresh oregano (or 2 tsp/10 mL dried)	50 mL
1/2 tsp	pepper	2 mL

● In large bowl, stir together flour, salt and baking powder. In separate bowl, whisk together oil, milk and 1 of the eggs; add to dry ingredients all at once. Using fingers or in mixer using dough hook, blend until liquid is absorbed and dough is smooth. Turn out onto lightly floured surface; knead for about 2 minutes or until velvety smooth. Transfer to bowl; cover and refrigerate for 30 minutes. (Pastry can be wrapped in plastic wrap and refrigerated for up to 5 days.)

● FILLING: Meanwhile, brush two large baking sheets with 2 tsp (10 mL) of the oil. Cut zucchini, onions and eggplant crosswise into 1/2-inch (1 cm) thick slices; place in single layer on prepared sheets. Brush with 2 tbsp (25 mL) of the oil; sprinkle with 1/2 tsp (2 mL) of the salt. Without peeling, separate garlic into cloves and place in small bowl; add remaining oil and toss to coat. Add garlic to sheets, reserving oil in bowl.

● Roast in 425°F (220°C) oven, rotating pans once, for about 40 minutes or until vegetables are tender and garlic is softened. Let cool. (Vegetables can be prepared to this point and refrigerated in airtight container for up to 12 hours.) Squeeze garlic from skins into reserved oil in bowl; mash with fork and set aside.

● On lightly floured surface or pastry cloth, roll out pastry to 18-inch (45 cm) circle; transfer to large baking sheet. Spread garlic in 9-inch (23 cm) circle in center of pastry. Top with one-third of the red peppers; sprinkle with one-third of the cheese, oregano, pepper and remaining salt. Repeat layers twice. Fold pastry border over filling to form attractive irregular edge, leaving 2-inch (5 cm) opening on top. Lightly beat remaining egg; brush over pastry to seal folds.

● Bake in lower third of 375°F (190°C) oven for about 30 minutes or until pastry is golden and filling is steaming. Let stand on sheet on rack for 5 minutes before cutting into wedges. Makes 6 servings.

ROASTING PEPPERS

Sweet red, yellow, orange and green peppers take on a wonderful smokiness when roasted or grilled. To grill, arrange on greased grill over medium-high heat; close lid and grill for about 20 minutes, turning every 5 minutes or until skin is charred and puffed. Or, broil for about the same time. Cover lightly and let rest for 10 minutes to further loosen the skin. Working over a sieve set atop a bowl, pull off skin and remove stem, membranes and seeds. Place peppers in bowl, saving juices from peeling process to help keep them moist. Peppers can be frozen with these juices in airtight containers or in freezer bag for up to 1 year. Use for pasta sauces, lasagna fillings, puréed in dips and in stews and soups. Or, dress with a vinaigrette and top with shaved Asiago or Parmesan cheese.

Broccoli Mushroom Quiche

	Pastry for 9-inch (23 cm) single-crust pie	
2-1/2 cups	broccoli florets	625 mL
1 tbsp	olive oil	15 mL
3 cups	sliced mushrooms (8 oz/250 g)	750 mL
1	sweet red pepper, chopped	1
1	onion, chopped	1
1 tsp	dried oregano	5 mL
1 lb	soft tofu	500 g
1/4 cup	chopped fresh parsley	50 mL
1	clove garlic, minced	1
1 tsp	salt	5 mL
1/4 tsp	pepper	1 mL

● On lightly floured surface, roll out pastry and fit into 9-inch (23 cm) pie plate; set aside.

● In large saucepan, cook broccoli in 1 inch (2.5 cm) boiling water for about 3 minutes or until tender-crisp; drain and set aside.

● In same saucepan, heat oil over medium heat; cover and cook mushrooms, red pepper, onion and oregano, stirring occasionally, for about 5 minutes or until onions are softened. Remove from heat. Add broccoli.

● In food processor, purée together tofu, parsley, garlic, salt and pepper; pour over broccoli mixture, stirring to combine. Spoon into prepared crust. Bake in 425°F (220°C) oven for 20 minutes. Reduce heat to 400°F (200°C); bake for about 30 minutes longer or until filling is set and pastry is golden. Let stand for 20 minutes before cutting into wedges. Makes 6 servings.

Tofu is an alternative to the usual eggs and milk in this supper dish.

Per serving: about
- 260 calories
- 10 g protein
- 16 g fat
- 21 g carbohydrate
- excellent source of iron

Rice with Red Pepper, Corn and Colby Cheese

3 cups	water	750 mL
1-1/2 cups	parboiled long-grain rice	375 mL
1/2 tsp	salt	2 mL
2 tbsp	butter	25 mL
1	large sweet red pepper, cored and seeded	1
2 cups	shredded Colby cheese (about 8 oz/250 g)	500 mL
1/2 cup	cooked corn kernels	125 mL
1/2 cup	sliced green onions	125 mL
1/4 tsp	hot pepper sauce	1 mL
1 cup	sour cream	250 mL
2/3 cup	freshly grated Parmesan cheese	150 mL
1/4 cup	coarse dry bread crumbs	50 ml

● In heavy saucepan, bring water to boil. Add rice and salt; reduce heat to low, cover and cook for about 25 minutes or until rice is tender and liquid absorbed. Stir in butter.

● Meanwhile, in small saucepan of boiling water, cook red pepper for 3 minutes or until skin loosens; let cool slightly. Peel and chop coarsely.

● Add red pepper, Colby cheese, corn, green onions and hot pepper sauce to rice; mix together. Transfer to shallow greased 8-cup (2 L) baking dish, pressing down gently. *(Recipe can be prepared to this point, covered and refrigerated for up to 1 day.)*

● Spread sour cream over rice mixture; sprinkle with Parmesan cheese and bread crumbs. Bake in 400°F (200°C) oven for 20 to 30 minutes or until heated through and topping is browned. Makes 6 servings.

Brick, Fontina, Friulano, Monterey Jack, Gouda and Swiss cheese can all be substituted for the Colby in this hearty dish.

Per serving: about
- 505 calories
- 20 g protein
- 25 g fat
- 49 g carbohydrate
- excellent source of calcium

Bulgur-Stuffed Acorn Squash for Two

Lemon, cumin and parsley brighten up the grain-and-chick-pea filling of this savory dish. For additional servings, simply double or triple the ingredients.

Per serving: about
- 325 calories
- 10 g protein
- 4 g fat
- 69 g carbohydrate
- very high source of fiber
- excellent source of iron

1	acorn squash or large sweet dumpling squash (2 lb/1 kg)	1
1 tsp	vegetable oil	5 mL
1/4 cup	each chopped onion and sweet green pepper	50 mL
1	clove garlic, minced	1
1/2 tsp	ground cumin	2 mL
1/3 cup	medium or coarse bulgur	75 mL
3/4 cup	hot vegetable stock	175 mL
1/2 cup	canned drained chick-peas	125 mL
1 tbsp	chopped fresh parsley	15 mL
1 tbsp	lemon juice	15 mL

● Halve and seed squash. Cut 1/2-inch (1 cm) thick slice from each cut side; peel and dice each slice. Set aside.

● Place squash, cut side down, on greased baking sheet. Bake in 400°F (200°C) oven for 40 to 45 minutes or until tender.

● Meanwhile, in saucepan, heat oil over medium heat; cook onion, green pepper, garlic and cumin, stirring occasionally, for about 3 minutes or until softened. Add bulgur and diced squash; cook, stirring, for 1 minute.

● Add stock and chick-peas; bring to boil. Cover and cook for 15 minutes or until liquid is absorbed and squash is tender. Stir in parsley and lemon juice. Keep warm.

● Turn squash over; spoon stuffing into each half. Cover with foil and bake for about 5 minutes or until heated through. Makes 2 servings.

Spaghetti Pizza Bake

Spaghetti, bound by an egg, holds children-pleasing pizza toppings. For tastebuds looking for more of a challenge, replace some of the mozzarella with a gutsier cheese such as provolone.

Per serving: about
- 340 calories
- 15 g protein
- 15 g fat
- 38 g carbohydrate
- good source of calcium

8 oz	spaghetti	250 g
2 tbsp	olive oil	25 mL
1/4 cup	freshly grated Parmesan cheese	50 mL
1	egg, beaten	1
1	onion, chopped	1
1	clove garlic, minced	1
2 cups	sliced mushrooms (about 6 oz/175 g)	500 mL
3/4 tsp	dried basil	4 mL
1/4 tsp	dried oregano	1 mL
1	can (14 oz/398 mL) tomato sauce	1
1-1/2 cups	shredded mozzarella cheese	375 mL
3/4 cup	chopped sweet green pepper	175 mL

● In large pot of boiling salted water, cook spaghetti for 8 to 10 minutes or until tender but firm; drain and transfer to bowl. Toss with 1 tbsp (15 mL) of the oil; let cool. Add Parmesan cheese and egg; toss to coat well. Press evenly over bottom and side of greased 9-inch (23 cm) pie plate.

● Meanwhile, in skillet, heat remaining oil over medium heat; cook onion, garlic, mushrooms, basil and oregano, stirring occasionally, for 5 minutes. Add tomato sauce; cook, stirring occasionally, for 10 minutes or until thickened.

● Sprinkle spaghetti mixture with 1/2 cup (125 mL) of the mozzarella cheese; spoon sauce over top. Sprinkle with green pepper and remaining mozzarella. Bake in 375°F (190°C) oven for 30 minutes or until spaghetti is golden brown. Let stand for 5 minutes. Makes 6 servings.

Layered Polenta and Ratatouille ▲

2 tbsp	olive oil	25 mL
2	small onions, sliced	2
1	clove garlic, minced	1
Half	sweet red pepper, chopped	Half
3 cups	diced eggplant	750 mL
1-1/2 cups	diced zucchini	375 mL
1-1/2 cups	canned tomatoes (undrained)	375 mL
3 tbsp	chopped fresh parsley	50 mL
1 tsp	vinegar	5 mL
1/2 tsp	each salt and dried rosemary	2 mL
1/4 tsp	each dried thyme and marjoram	1 mL
Pinch	pepper	Pinch
1/2 cup	shredded Asiago	125 mL
	POLENTA	
4 cups	water	1 L
1/2 tsp	salt	2 mL
1 cup	cornmeal	250 mL

● In large saucepan, heat oil over medium heat; cook onions and garlic, stirring occasionally, for about 5 minutes or until softened. Add red pepper; cook, stirring, for about 2 minutes or until tender-crisp.

● Add eggplant and zucchini; cook, stirring often, for 10 minutes or until softened. Stir in tomatoes, breaking up with spoon. Add parsley, vinegar, salt, rosemary, thyme, marjoram and pepper. Remove from heat.

● POLENTA: In saucepan, bring water and salt to boil; whisk in cornmeal. Cook over medium-low heat, stirring, for 20 to 25 minutes or until polenta mounds on spoon.

● Spread half of the polenta in greased 9-inch (2.5 L) square cake pan; top with eggplant mixture, spreading evenly. Spread with remaining polenta; sprinkle with cheese.

● Bake in 350°F (180°C) oven for 40 minutes or until filling is hot and top is browned. Let stand for 10 minutes. Makes 4 servings.

W*ho wouldn't enjoy this robust eggplant, zucchini and tomato stew baked between layers of polenta! Substitute mozzarella for Asiago, if desired.*

Per serving: about
- 300 calories
- 12 g fat
- high source of fiber
- 8 g protein
- 42 g carbohydrate
- good source of calcium

Simmers and Skillets

Today's hectic pace calls for creativity in the kitchen. Easy simmering chilis, stews and soups when there's make-ahead time, or quick stove-top suppers when the rush is on, are the answer.

Black Bean and Vegetable Chili ▶

A *pressure cooker speeds up the usually long soaking time that legumes require. Spoon this chili over mounds of hot rice and sprinkle with shredded old Cheddar cheese.*

Per serving: about
- 390 calories
- 15 g fat
- very high source of fiber
- 15 g protein
- 53 g carbohydrate
- excellent source of iron

1 cup	dried black beans, rinsed	250 mL
1 tbsp	vegetable oil	15 mL
3 tbsp	olive oil	50 mL
2	cloves garlic, minced	2
2	stalks celery, sliced	2
2	large carrots, diced	2
1 cup	each diced zucchini, onions, mushrooms and sweet red or green pepper	250 mL
1	can (28 oz/796 mL) tomatoes (undrained), chopped	1
1-1/2 cups	water or vegetable stock	375 mL
1/2 cup	chopped fresh parsley	125 mL
1 tbsp	chili powder	15 mL
1 tsp	each dried basil and oregano	5 mL
1 tsp	each salt and ground cumin	5 mL
1/2 tsp	pepper	2 mL

● In pressure cooker, combine 4 cups (1 L) salted water, black beans and vegetable oil. Secure lid; bring to High pressure over high heat. Reduce heat to just maintain High pressure; cook for 2 minutes. Let pressure release quickly under cold running water. Drain and rinse beans; set aside.

● In cooker, heat olive oil over medium heat; cook garlic, celery, carrots, zucchini, onions, mushrooms and red pepper, stirring often, for about 7 minutes or until softened.

● Add black beans, tomatoes, water, parsley, chili powder, basil, oregano, salt, cumin and pepper. Secure lid; bring to High pressure over high heat. Reduce heat to just maintain High pressure and cook for 20 minutes. Remove from heat; let stand until pressure is completely released, 8 to 10 minutes. Makes 4 servings.

STORING VEGETABLES

To store tender vegetables such as carrots, celery, parsley and peppers, loosely wrap in towels before enclosing in plastic bags and placing in refrigerator. Paper towels are handy, but clean kitchen towels are equally good. Tomatoes should be ripened at room temperature out of sunlight and refrigerated only if they threaten to spoil. Onions should be kept in a cool, dry, dark spot. Mushrooms should be stored in paper, never plastic, bags.

Vegetarian Chili in Sweet Potato Boats ▲

Sweet potatoes — which have just about the same number of calories as regular white potatoes — readily hold a ladleful of chili. The cozy combo makes fine entertaining fare.

Per serving: about
- 360 calories
- 4 g fat
- very high source of fiber
- 11 g protein
- 74 g carbohydrate
- excellent source of iron

6	large sweet potatoes	6
1 tbsp	olive oil	15 mL
2	sweet green peppers, diced	2
2	onions, chopped	2
2	cloves garlic, minced	2
1 tbsp	chili powder	15 mL
2 tsp	ground cumin	10 mL
1 tsp	ground coriander	5 mL
1/2 tsp	salt	2 mL
1/4 tsp	pepper	1 mL
1	can (28 oz/796 mL) tomatoes, chopped	1
1	can (14 oz/398 mL) black beans, drained and rinsed	1
1 cup	corn kernels	250 mL
1/4 cup	chopped fresh coriander or parsley	50 mL
1/3 cup	plain yogurt	75 mL
	Lime wedges	

● Place sweet potatoes on baking sheet; pierce all over with fork. Bake in 400°F (200°C) oven for about 1 hour and 25 minutes or until tender.

● Meanwhile, in large nonstick skillet, heat oil over medium heat; cook green peppers, onions, garlic, chili powder, cumin, coriander, salt and pepper, stirring occasionally, for 10 minutes.

● Stir in tomatoes and beans; bring to boil. Reduce heat, cover and simmer for 20 minutes. Stir in corn and half of the coriander; cook, uncovered, for 5 minutes.

● Place sweet potatoes on plates; slit lengthwise through middle and mash insides with fork. With back of spoon, press hollows in potatoes; spoon in chili. Top with spoonful of yogurt; sprinkle with remaining coriander. Garnish with lime. Makes 6 servings.

Meal-in-a-Spud

2	baking potatoes	2
1-1/2 cups	spaghetti sauce	375 mL
1/2 cup	diced zucchini	125 mL
1/4 cup	canned white kidney or lima beans	50 mL
1/2 tsp	dried oregano	2 mL
Pinch	each salt and pepper	Pinch
2 oz	firm tofu, cut in 3/4-inch (2 cm) cubes	60 g

● Prick potatoes all over with fork. Microwave at High for 6 minutes, or bake in 400°F (200°C) oven for 45 to 60 minutes, or until tender. Place each in shallow bowl. Cut in half lengthwise almost but not all the way through; fluff up flesh with fork.

● Meanwhile, in saucepan, combine spaghetti sauce, zucchini, beans, oregano, salt and pepper; cook over medium heat for about 5 minutes or until zucchini is tender. Add tofu; cook for 1 minute or until heated through. Spoon over potatoes. Makes 2 servings.

The carbohydrates in potatoes make them the food of contentment. Add a protein-rich tofu-, vegetable-and-bean topping for sustaining power and an impressively easy meal.

Per serving: about
- 400 calories
- 8 g fat
- very high source of fiber
- 13 g protein
- 72 g carbohydrate
- excellent source of iron

Creamy Pearl Barley and Vegetable Risotto

6 cups	vegetable stock	1.5 L
1-1/2 cups	dry white wine or vegetable stock	375 mL
1-3/4 cups	pearl barley	425 mL
1 tbsp	olive oil	15 mL
2 cups	sliced mushrooms (about 6 oz/175 g)	500 mL
1	onion, chopped	1
1	clove garlic, minced	1
2 cups	diced peeled sweet potato	500 mL
1 tsp	dried thyme (or 1 tbsp/15 mL chopped fresh)	5 mL
3 cups	small broccoli florets	750 mL
Pinch	each salt and pepper	Pinch
1/2 cup	freshly grated Parmesan cheese	125 mL

● Combine stock and wine. In large heavy saucepan, combine 3-1/2 cups (875 mL) of the stock mixture and barley; cover and bring to boil. Reduce heat to medium-low; simmer, stirring occasionally, for 25 to 30 minutes or until almost all liquid is absorbed.

● Stir in 3 cups (750 mL) of the stock mixture, 1/2 cup (125 mL) at a time, cooking and stirring constantly until each addition is absorbed before adding next, until barley is tender and creamy, about 25 minutes. Remove from heat; cover and set aside.

● Meanwhile, in large saucepan, heat oil over medium heat; cook mushrooms, onion and garlic, stirring often, for 5 to 10 minutes or until mushrooms are softened.

● Stir in remaining stock mixture, sweet potato and thyme; cover and simmer over medium-low heat for 8 minutes, stirring occasionally. Add broccoli; cook for 6 to 8 minutes or until vegetables are tender. Stir in barley mixture, salt and pepper until hot throughout. Serve sprinkled with Parmesan cheese. Makes 5 servings.

Barley retains a bit of crunch, even in a risotto. This recipe is adapted from a barley risotto served at Capers, a Vancouver restaurant with a reputation for good-tasting, good-for-you food.

Per serving: about
- 440 calories
- 8 g fat
- very high source of fiber
- excellent source of iron
- 13 g protein
- 78 g carbohydrate
- good source of calcium

Harvest Risotto

Using short-grain Arborio rice is the secret to making a creamy, comfy risotto. Serve in bowls, together with a side salad of tomatoes and lettuce.

Per serving: about
- 560 calories
- 20 g fat
- high source of fiber
- 16 g protein
- 80 g carbohydrate
- excellent source of calcium

2 tbsp	olive oil	25 mL
2 tbsp	butter	25 mL
1	onion, chopped	1
2	cloves garlic, minced	2
1 cup	sliced mushrooms	250 mL
1	zucchini, cut in large dice	1
1	sweet red pepper, diced	1
1 cup	cooked corn kernels	250 mL
1 tsp	chopped fresh rosemary	5 mL
1/4 tsp	pepper (approx)	1 mL
Pinch	salt (approx)	Pinch
Pinch	hot pepper flakes	Pinch
1-1/2 cups	Arborio rice	375 mL
1 tbsp	grated lemon rind	15 mL
4-1/2 cups	vegetable stock	1.125 L
3/4 cup	freshly grated Parmesan cheese	175 mL
1 tbsp	lemon juice	15 mL

● In large heavy saucepan, heat half each of the oil and butter over medium heat; cook onion, garlic and mushrooms, stirring occasionally, for 5 minutes or until softened.

● Add zucchini, red pepper, corn, rosemary, pepper, salt and hot pepper flakes; cook, stirring, for 3 to 5 minutes or until liquid is evaporated. Remove from pan; keep warm.

● Add remaining oil and butter to pan over medium-high heat; cook rice and lemon rind, stirring, for 1 minute. Stir in 1/2 cup (125 mL) of the stock; cook, stirring constantly, until all liquid is absorbed. Keep adding stock, 1/2 cup (125 mL) at a time, cooking and stirring until each addition is absorbed before adding next, until rice is tender, about 18 minutes.

● Stir in 1/2 cup (125 mL) of the Parmesan cheese, lemon juice and vegetable mixture; heat through. Season with more salt and pepper to taste. Sprinkle with remaining cheese. Makes 4 servings.

Wild Mushroom Risotto

Purists may prefer the classic method of stirring constantly when making a risotto, but stirring less often — as in this recipe — produces a velvety risotto, too.

Per serving: about
- 465 calories
- 15 g fat
- good source of calcium
- 12 g protein
- 70 g carbohydrate

6 cups	vegetable stock	1.5 L
1 oz	dried porcini or shiitake mushrooms	30 g
1 tbsp	olive oil	15 mL
2 tbsp	butter	25 mL
1	onion, finely chopped	1
1-1/2 cups	Arborio rice	375 mL
1/2 cup	freshly grated Parmesan cheese	125 mL
1/4 cup	minced fresh parsley	50 mL
Pinch	each salt and pepper	Pinch

● Bring stock to boil; remove from heat. Add mushrooms; let stand for 20 minutes or until soft. With slotted spoon, remove mushrooms and squeeze out liquid; pat dry and chop. Set aside. Strain liquid through cheesecloth or coffee filter to remove grit; set aside.

● In large nonstick skillet, heat oil and half of the butter over medium heat; cook onion, stirring often, for 3 minutes.

● Add reserved soaking liquid; bring to boil. Add rice; simmer over medium heat for 15 minutes or until liquid is almost evaporated and rice is creamy but still firm, adding boiling water to thin risotto if desired.

● Stir in mushrooms; heat through. Stir in remaining butter, Parmesan cheese, parsley, salt and pepper. Makes 4 servings.

TIP: Porcini, morels and shiitake reign supreme among dried mushrooms. Other varieties are often just as expensive, but they lack the woodsy flavor we expect in a wild mushroom.

Primavera Risotto ▼

1 lb	asparagus	500 g
1	sweet yellow or red pepper	1
2	carrots	2
4-3/4 cups	vegetable stock	1.175 L
2 tbsp	olive oil	25 mL
1	onion, chopped	1
2	cloves garlic, minced	2
2 tsp	grated lemon rind	10 mL
1 tsp	dried thyme (or 1 tbsp/15 mL fresh)	5 mL
1/4 tsp	each salt and pepper	1 mL
1-1/2 cups	Arborio rice	375 mL
3/4 cup	white wine	175 mL
1 cup	frozen peas	250 mL
1/2 cup	freshly grated Parmesan cheese	125 mL

● Holding each asparagus spear at base and halfway up stalk, bend just until stalk snaps at natural breaking point; reserve bases for another use. Cut stalks into 1-inch (2.5 cm) pieces. Cut yellow pepper into bite-size chunks. Cut carrots diagonally into thin slices. Set vegetables aside separately.

● In saucepan, bring stock just to simmer; reduce heat to low and keep warm. In separate large shallow saucepan, heat oil over medium heat; cook onion and garlic, stirring often, for 3 minutes or until softened. Stir in lemon rind, thyme, salt and pepper. Add rice and carrots, stirring until well coated.

● Stir in 1/2 cup (125 mL) of the stock; cook, stirring constantly, until liquid is absorbed. Stir in wine; cook, stirring, until wine is

absorbed. Keep adding stock, 1/2 cup (125 mL) at a time, cooking and stirring until each addition is absorbed before adding next, about 15 minutes.

● Stir in asparagus and yellow pepper. Continue stirring and adding stock, 1/2 cup (125 mL) at a time, for 10 to 15 minutes or until rice is tender and asparagus is tender-crisp. Stir in peas, cheese and any remaining stock; cook, stirring, for 2 minutes or until risotto is very creamy but still fluid. Makes 4 servings.

Y ou can moisten the rice in risotto solely with stock, but a generous splash of white wine adds such an unforgettable rich flavor that you must try it in this special-occasion springtime entrée.

Per serving: about
- 530 calories
- 21 g protein
- 13 g fat
- 78 g carbohydrate
- good source of calcium and iron
- high source of fiber

Curried Vegetables with Bulgur

Although this is a simmered curry, it is fresh-tasting because the vegetables are cooked just to tender-crisp and a sprig of fresh mint is added to each serving,

Per serving: about
• 425 calories
• 16 g protein
• 10 g fat
• 75 g carbohydrate
• very high source of fiber
• excellent source of iron

1-1/2 cups	bulgur	375 mL
2 tbsp	vegetable oil	25 mL
1/2 cup	chopped green onions	125 mL
2	cloves garlic, minced	2
2	carrots, diced	2
2	stalks celery, diced	2
1 tbsp	dried coriander	15 mL
2 tsp	ground cumin	10 mL
1 tsp	each turmeric and salt	5 mL
1/2 tsp	pepper	2 mL
Pinch	cayenne pepper	Pinch
1	can (19 oz/540 mL) chick-peas, drained and rinsed	1
2	zucchini, diced	2
2	tomatoes, diced	2
1 tbsp	lemon juice	15 mL
2 tbsp	chopped fresh mint	25 mL

● In large bowl, cover bulgur with boiling water; let stand for 30 minutes. Drain well in sieve, pressing to extract excess water.

● Meanwhile, in nonstick skillet, heat oil over medium-high heat; cook onions, garlic, carrots and celery, stirring occasionally, for about 5 minutes or until softened.

● Stir in coriander, cumin, turmeric, salt, pepper and cayenne; cook, stirring, for 1 minute. Stir in chick-peas, zucchini, tomatoes and lemon juice; bring to boil. Reduce heat to medium; cook for about 5 minutes or until vegetables are tender-crisp.

● Divide bulgur among 4 plates; top with vegetable mixture. Sprinkle with mint. Makes 4 servings.

Skillet Vegetable Stew

Just summer vegetables, but they're oh, so delicious in this quick stew that begs for a crusty roll and a toss of greens to finish it.

Per serving: about
• 240 calories
• 8 g protein
• 6 g fat
• 43 g carbohydrate
• very high source of fiber
• good source of iron

1 tbsp	olive oil	15 mL
Half	onion, sliced	Half
3	tomatoes, coarsely chopped	3
1-1/2 tsp	salt	7 mL
1 tsp	each dried basil and pepper	5 mL
4	red potatoes, cut in 1/2-inch (1 cm) cubes	4
1	sweet red or green pepper, chopped	1
2 cups	each cubed eggplant and zucchini	500 mL
1/4 cup	chopped fresh parsley	50 mL
1/4 cup	freshly grated Parmesan cheese	50 mL

● In large nonstick skillet, heat oil over medium heat; cook onion, stirring occasionally, for 5 minutes or until softened. Add tomatoes, salt, basil and pepper; cover and cook for 5 minutes.

● Add potatoes, 1/4 cup (50 mL) water and red pepper; bring to boil. Reduce heat and simmer, covered, for 10 minutes. Stir in eggplant; simmer, covered and stirring occasionally, for 10 minutes.

● Add zucchini; cook, covered, for about 5 minutes or until zucchini is tender-crisp and other vegetables are tender. Stir in parsley. Serve sprinkled with Parmesan cheese. Makes 4 servings.

TIP: If you have fresh basil, use 1/4 cup (50 mL) chopped instead of the dried basil and fresh parsley.

Vegetable Paella ▲

1 tbsp	olive oil	15 mL
1	large onion, chopped	1
1	sweet red pepper, thinly sliced	1
2	carrots, chopped	2
1-1/2 cups	sliced mushrooms	375 mL
1-1/2 cups	long-grain rice	375 mL
1/4 tsp	crumbled saffron	1 mL
3	cloves garlic, minced	3
3 cups	vegetable stock	750 mL
1 cup	cut (2-inch/5 cm) green beans	250 mL
1/4 cup	chopped sun-dried tomatoes	50 mL
1/4 tsp	each salt and pepper	1 mL
1 cup	cooked chick-peas	250 mL
1/2 cup	frozen peas	125 mL
2 tbsp	lemon juice	25 mL
4	hard-cooked eggs	4

● In large skillet, heat oil over medium heat; cook onion, red pepper, carrots and mushrooms, stirring often, for 10 minutes or until starting to brown. Add rice, saffron and garlic; cook, stirring, for 2 minutes.

● Stir in stock, green beans, tomatoes, salt and pepper; cover and simmer for about 17 minutes or until rice is tender.

● Stir in chick-peas, frozen peas and lemon juice. Cut eggs into wedges; arrange over top. Cook, covered, for 1 to 2 minutes or until hot. Makes 4 servings.

Especially for novice cooks, this fiber- and iron-rich rice dish has all the flair of its Spanish origins, but uses ingredients you can find in any supermarket.

Per serving: about
- 520 calories
- 11 g fat
- very high source of fiber
- 19 g protein
- 86 g carbohydrate
- excellent source of iron

Lentil Curry with Squash and Spinach

The tantalizing aroma of this inexpensive, high-fiber dish is sure to bring everyone to the table on time. Serve with rice, warm pita or naan breads, and thick yogurt.

Per serving: about
- 220 calories
- 4 g fat
- very high source of fiber
- 12 g protein
- 39 g carbohydrate
- excellent source of iron

1 tbsp	vegetable oil	15 mL
1	onion, chopped	1
2	cloves garlic, minced	2
2 tbsp	all-purpose flour	25 mL
1 tbsp	each curry powder and grated gingerroot	15 mL
1 tsp	each ground cumin and fennel seeds	5 mL
2-1/2 cups	vegetable stock	625 mL
1-1/2 cups	water	375 mL
1 cup	green lentils	250 mL
1	large potato	1
Half	butternut squash (1 lb/500 g)	Half
6 cups	fresh spinach	1.5 L

● In large heavy saucepan, heat oil over medium heat; cook onion and garlic, stirring often, for 5 minutes or until softened.

● Sprinkle with flour, curry powder, ginger, cumin and fennel seeds; cook, stirring, for 1 minute. Add stock, water and lentils; bring to boil. Cover, reduce heat and simmer for 30 minutes.

● Meanwhile, peel and cut potato into 3/4-inch (2 cm) cubes; add to pan. Cover and cook for 10 minutes. Meanwhile, peel and seed squash; cut into 3/4-inch (2 cm) cubes. Stir into pan; cook, uncovered, for about 15 minutes or until tender and liquid is thickened.

● Trim and coarsely chop spinach; add to pan and cook, stirring, until wilted. Makes 6 servings.

Grilled Tofu Skewers

Firm tofu is much easier to grill or stir-fry than the softer versions and is now widely available in supermarkets. A zesty marinade is the perfect flavor enhancer (drizzle any leftovers on the tofu). Serve with rice.

Per serving: about
- 200 calories
- 12 g fat
- high source of fiber
- excellent source of iron
- 19 g protein
- 9 g carbohydrate
- good source of calcium

1 lb	firm tofu	500 g
1/4 cup	soy sauce	50 mL
1/4 cup	red wine (or 2 tbsp/ 25 mL red wine vinegar)	50 mL
3 tbsp	rice vinegar	50 mL
1 tbsp	sesame oil	15 mL
1/2 tsp	chili paste (or dash hot pepper sauce)	2 mL
2	cloves garlic, minced	2
1	small zucchini	1
1	sweet red or yellow pepper	1

● Drain tofu and place in deep dish; cover with plate and weigh down with heavy can. Let stand for 1 hour. Pat tofu dry; cut into twelve 1-inch (2.5 cm) thick chunks. Place in shallow dish.

● Whisk together soy sauce, wine, vinegar, oil, chili paste and garlic; pour over tofu. Cover and refrigerate, turning occasionally, for at least 8 hours or for up to 24 hours.

● Cut zucchini and red pepper into eight 1-inch (2.5 cm) pieces. Onto each of four skewers, thread piece of tofu lengthwise, reserving marinade, then piece of zucchini and sweet pepper. Repeat once, ending with final piece of tofu.

● Place on greased grill over medium-high heat; close lid and cook, turning once and basting occasionally with reserved marinade, for 8 to 10 minutes or until browned. Makes 4 servings.

The Pleasure of a Pilaf

Each half cup (125 mL) of these grain side dishes provides one of the five to twelve servings of grain products per day recommended by Canada's Food Guide. Help yourself to more than one serving to meet the needed total and satisfy your hunger.

PICK-A-GRAIN PILAF

1 tbsp	vegetable oil	15 mL
1	onion, chopped	1
1/2 tsp	dried tarragon	2 mL
1 cup	bulgur	250 mL
2 cups	vegetable stock or water	500 mL
1/4 tsp	salt	1 mL
1	large carrot, grated	1
1/2 cup	frozen peas	125 mL
1 tbsp	lemon juice	15 ml
1/4 tsp	pepper	1 mL

● In small heavy saucepan, heat oil over medium-high heat; cook onion and tarragon, stirring occasionally, for 3 minutes or until softened. Add bulgur; cook, stirring, for 1 minute.

● Add stock and salt; bring to boil. Reduce heat to low; cover and simmer for 20 minutes.

● With fork, stir in carrot and peas; cook, covered, for 5 minutes or until carrot and bulgur are tender and liquid is absorbed. Add lemon juice and pepper; toss with fork. Makes 4 servings.

Per serving: about
• 205 calories • 8 g protein • 5 g fat • 35 g carbohydrate
• very high source of fiber • good source of iron

VARIATIONS
● RICE PILAF: Substitute white rice for bulgur and dried oregano for tarragon.

● BARLEY PILAF: Substitute barley for bulgur and dried savory for tarragon; increase cooking time to about 50 minutes.

● COUSCOUS PILAF: Substitute couscous for bulgur and dried basil for tarragon. Decrease stock to 1-1/2 cups (375 mL). Cook onions and basil as above. Add stock, salt, carrot and peas; bring to boil. Stir in couscous; cover, remove from heat and let stand for 5 minutes. Add lemon juice and pepper; fluff with fork.

QUINOA PILAF

1 tbsp	olive oil	15 mL
Half	onion, chopped	Half
1	stalk celery (including leaves), diced	1
2	carrots, finely chopped	2
1/2 cup	quinoa	125 mL
1 cup	hot water or vegetable stock	250 mL
1	bay leaf	1
1 tbsp	each grated lemon rind and juice	15 mL
1/2 cup	frozen peas, thawed	125 mL
Pinch	each salt and pepper	Pinch

● In saucepan, heat oil over medium heat; cook onion, celery and carrots, stirring often, for 10 minutes.

● In strainer, rinse quinoa under cold water; drain well and add to pan. Cook, stirring, for 1 minute.

● Add water, bay leaf and lemon rind and juice; bring to boil. Reduce heat to medium-low; cover and simmer for 15 to 20 minutes or until liquid is absorbed and quinoa is tender. Discard bay leaf. Stir in peas; season with salt and pepper. Makes 3 servings.

Per serving: about
• 200 calories • 6 g protein • 6 g fat • 31 g carbohydrate
• high source of fiber • good source of iron

TIP: The grainlike quinoa, available in health food stores and some supermarkets, has a mild flavor, so serve it as you would rice or other grains — with stews, stir-fries or in salads.

Tuscan Kidney Beans with Sage

*H*ere's a dish that's a snap
to put together using canned
beans, and one you can serve
with grilled or steamed
vegetables and crusty bread
for a year-round dinner. The
robust flavor of the sage
complements the earthiness
of the beans.

Per serving: about
• 160 calories • 8 g protein
• 4 g fat • 23 g carbohydrate
• very high source
  of fiber

2	tomatoes, coarsely chopped	2
1 tbsp	chopped fresh sage (or 1 tsp/5 mL crumbled dried)	15 mL
1	clove garlic, minced	1
1	can (19 oz/540 mL) white kidney beans, drained and rinsed	1
1 tbsp	extra-virgin olive oil	15 mL
1 tbsp	red wine vinegar	15 mL
Pinch	each salt and pepper	Pinch

● In large saucepan, stir together tomatoes, sage and garlic; simmer over medium heat for about 20 minutes or until liquid is evaporated.

● Add beans; cook, stirring, for about 5 minutes or until hot. Remove from heat.

● Stir together oil, vinegar, salt and pepper; stir into bean mixture. Makes 4 servings.

Watercress Frittata ▶

*W*atercress has a nippy edge
that does wonders for the
mild and mellow flavors of
eggs and mozzarella cheese.

Per serving: about
• 255 calories • 19 g protein
• 18 g fat • 4 g carbohydrate
• excellent source
  of calcium

4	eggs	4
2	egg whites	2
1/3 cup	freshly grated Parmesan cheese	75 mL
1/2 tsp	salt	2 mL
Pinch	pepper	Pinch
1	bunch watercress	1
1 tbsp	olive oil	15 mL
1 cup	sliced mushrooms	250 mL
2	cloves garlic, minced	2
2	green onions, sliced	2
1/2 tsp	dried basil	2 mL
4 oz	mozzarella cheese, cut in thin strips	125 g

● In bowl, whisk together eggs, egg whites, 1/4 cup (50 mL) of the Parmesan cheese, salt and pepper; set aside. Remove enough watercress leaves to measure 1 cup (250 mL) packed; discard stems and set remaining sprigs aside for garnish.

● In large ovenproof skillet, heat oil over medium-high heat; cook mushrooms, garlic, onions and basil, stirring often, for about 3 minutes or until mushrooms are lightly browned. Add watercress; cook, stirring often, for about 2 minutes or until wilted.

● Remove from heat. Stir in remaining Parmesan cheese; spread evenly over bottom of skillet. Pour egg mixture over top; cook over medium heat for 1 minute.

● Sprinkle with mozzarella cheese; place under broiler and broil until cheese begins to brown, 2 to 3 minutes. Slide onto warm serving plate; garnish with watercress sprigs. Cut into wedges to serve. Makes 4 servings.

Ricotta and Spinach Frittata

Roll this frittata in leaf lettuce, or pop — cold or hot — into a pita half with a little Dijon mustard, light mayonnaise and lettuce, and call it supper. It also makes satisfying lunchbox fare.

Per serving: about
- 145 calories
- 9 g protein
- 11 g fat
- 4 g carbohydrate

1	onion, chopped	1
2 tbsp	olive oil	25 mL
1/2 cup	ricotta cheese	125 mL
1	pkg (300 g) frozen chopped spinach, thawed and squeezed dry	1
1/3 cup	freshly grated Parmesan cheese	75 mL
1/2 tsp	each dried basil and salt	2 mL
1/4 tsp	pepper	1 mL
Pinch	nutmeg	Pinch
6	eggs	6
8	leaves Boston lettuce	8

● In 9-inch (23 cm) pie plate, toss onion with oil; bake in 400°F (200°C) oven for 10 minutes. In bowl, mix together ricotta, spinach, Parmesan cheese, basil, salt, pepper, nutmeg and eggs; stir in onion.

● Brush oil remaining in pie plate up side of plate; pour in egg mixture. Bake in 400°F (200°C) oven for 20 to 25 minutes or just until center is set. Let cool.

● Cut frittata into 8 wedges. Wrap each in lettuce leaf. *(Each serving can be wrapped in plastic wrap and refrigerated for up to 1 day.)* Makes 8 servings.

Solo Frittata

The microwave oven, ideal for cooking for one or two, makes a delectable vegetable-rich frittata.

Per serving: about
- 280 calories
- 18 g protein
- 19 g fat
- 8 g carbohydrate
- good source of calcium and iron

1 tsp	butter	5 mL
1 tbsp	chopped onion	15 mL
4	stalks asparagus, cut diagonally in 1-inch (2.5 cm) lengths	4
2	eggs	2
1 tbsp	crushed cracker crumbs	15 mL
Pinch	each salt and pepper	Pinch
2 tbsp	shredded Cheddar cheese	25 mL

● In lightly greased 2-cup (500 mL) microwaveable dish, microwave butter with onion at High for 30 seconds. Add asparagus; cover and cook at High for 30 seconds.

● In small bowl, beat eggs lightly; stir in crumbs, salt and pepper. Pour over asparagus; cook, uncovered, at Medium (50% power), stirring halfway through, for 1 to 2 minutes or until just set in center. Sprinkle with cheese; cover and let stand for 5 minutes. Makes 1 serving.

EGGS-TRAVAGANZA

Is it any wonder some people call the egg nature's perfect food? Economical, delicious and easy to prepare, eggs contribute to our diets in many ways. They're an inexpensive source of high-quality protein, and a source of vitamins B12, E, riboflavin and folacin, and the minerals iron and phosphorus. According to *Canada's Food Guide to* *Healthy Eating*, one to two eggs provides one serving from the meat and alternatives food groups. Store eggs in their original carton in the coldest part of the refrigerator (not in the door, which is usually warmer than the rest of the fridge), and keep away from strong-smelling foods (the phosphorus shell absorbs odors).

Corn and Zucchini Pancakes

1-1/3 cups	all-purpose flour	325 mL
1 tbsp	granulated sugar	15 mL
1 tbsp	baking powder	15 mL
1/2 tsp	salt	2 mL
1	egg	1
1 cup	milk	250 mL
1 tbsp	vegetable oil	15 mL
3/4 cup	cooked corn kernels	175 mL
1/3 cup	shredded zucchini	75 mL

● In large bowl, stir together flour, sugar, baking powder and salt. Whisk together egg, milk and oil; pour over dry ingredients. Sprinkle with corn and zucchini; stir just until dry ingredients are moistened.

● Heat large nonstick skillet over medium heat; brush with oil. Using 1/4 cup (50 mL) batter for each pancake and brushing skillet lightly with oil as necessary, cook pancakes for about 2 minutes or until golden brown on bottom and bubbles break on top but do not fill in. Turn and cook for about 45 seconds or until bottoms are golden brown. Makes twelve 3-inch (8 cm) pancakes.

VARIATION
● APPLE PANCAKES: Substitute 1 cup (250 mL) grated apple for corn and zucchini.

In summer, cook up a few extra cobs one day to make these colorful supper pancakes the next day. The rest of the year, substitute canned or thawed frozen corn, both well drained, and top with low-fat yogurt, salsa or syrup.

Per pancake: about
• 100 calories   • 3 g protein
• 3 g fat   • 15 g carbohydrate

TIP: These pancakes can be frozen for up to two weeks if wrapped well in plastic wrap and enclosed in a freezer bag. Pop them in the toaster oven for a busy-morning breakfast, after-school snack or quick supper.

Golden Squash Pancakes

1	squash (1 lb/500 g)	1
1/4 cup	chopped green onion	50 mL
1	egg	1
2 tbsp	all-purpose flour	25 mL
1/4 tsp	each salt and dried thyme	1 mL
Pinch	pepper	Pinch
	Vegetable oil for skillet	

● Peel and seed squash; grate to make about 3 cups (750 mL). *(Squash can be refrigerated in airtight container for up to 8 hours.)* Pat squash dry.

● In large bowl, whisk together onion, egg, flour, salt, thyme and pepper; stir in squash.

● Heat large nonstick skillet over medium heat; brush with oil. Using 1/4 cup (50 mL) packed squash mixture per pancake, drop into pan. Flatten with spatula to 1/2-inch (1 cm) thickness; cook for about 2 minutes or until golden. Turn and cook for about 3 minutes longer or until golden brown and crisp. Transfer to baking sheet; place in 250°F (120°C) oven to keep warm. Repeat with remaining mixture. Makes about 8 pancakes, or 4 servings.

Brunch, supper or lunch — take your pick for these savory pancakes. Round off the menu with a green-bean or Greek salad.

Per pancake: about
• 70 calories   • 3 g protein
• 1 g fat   • 12 g carbohydrate

TIP: Delicata and butternut squash, both dense and dry, are best for pancakes.

Vegetable Legume and Barley Soup

*H*ats off to the University
Women's Club of Vancouver
for creating this vegetable
soup mix they sell at their
annual Christmas at Hycroft.
It simmers up into this
delicious, sustaining soup.

Per serving: about
- 295 calories
- 1 g fat
- very high source of fiber
- 16 g protein
- 58 g carbohydrate
- excellent source of iron

2-1/2 cups	Vegetarian Soup Mix (recipe follows)	625 mL
1	onion, chopped	1
1	stalk celery, chopped	1
3/4 tsp	salt	4 mL
1/2 tsp	pepper	2 mL
1	bottle (28 oz/796 mL) vegetable juice cocktail or tomato juice	1

● In large heavy saucepan, combine soup mix, onion, celery, 7 cups (1.75 L) water, salt and pepper; bring to boil. Reduce heat, cover and simmer, stirring often, for about 40 minutes or until thickened and peas, lentils and barley are tender. Stir in vegetable juice cocktail; heat through. Makes 6 servings.

VEGETARIAN SOUP MIX		
2 cups	split peas (green, yellow or mixed)	500 mL
1 cup	red lentils	250 mL
1 cup	dried vegetable flakes	250 mL
1 cup	pearl barley	250 mL
2 tbsp	dried parsley	25 mL
2 tbsp	dried vegetable stock mix	25 mL
1 tbsp	dried basil	15 mL
1/2 tsp	salt	2 mL

● Stir together peas, lentils, dried vegetable flakes, barley, parsley, stock mix, basil and salt. Store in airtight container in cool, dry place. Makes about 5 cups (1.25 L), enough for 2 batches of soup.

TIPS
● Busy bulk-food stores offer the greatest variety of fresh grains and legumes.
● Keep this handy in airtight containers in a cool, dry, dark spot.

Tortellini Bean Soup

*W*ith a package of cheese-
filled tortellini tucked away
in the freezer, you can always
rustle up a tasty and
nourishing supper. Top with
pasta sauce or pop into a
rib-sticking vegetable soup.

Per serving: about
- 355 calories
- 9 g fat
- very high source of fiber
- 17 g protein
- 54 g carbohydrate
- good source of calcium and iron

2 tsp	vegetable oil	10 mL
4	carrots, chopped	4
1	onion, chopped	1
2	cloves garlic, minced	2
1 tsp	dried basil	5 mL
1	bay leaf	1
3 cups	vegetable stock	750 mL
1	can (19 oz/540 mL) tomatoes	1
8 oz	fresh cheese-filled tortellini	250 g
1 cup	rinsed drained canned black beans	250 mL
1/4 tsp	pepper	1 mL
1/4 cup	freshly grated Parmesan cheese	50 mL

● In large heavy saucepan, heat oil over medium heat; cook carrots, onion, garlic, basil and bay leaf, stirring occasionally, for about 5 minutes or until onion is softened.

● Add stock and tomatoes, breaking up with back of spoon; bring to boil. Add tortellini; return to boil. Reduce heat to medium-high; cook, stirring occasionally, for about 10 minutes or until pasta is almost tender but firm.

● Stir in beans and season with pepper; heat until simmering. Discard bay leaf. Ladle into bowls; sprinkle with Parmesan cheese. Makes 4 servings.

TIP: Any leftover canned beans can be added to a salad or stirred into a rice pilaf.

Mexican Black Bean Soup ▼

3 cups	black beans	750 mL
1 tbsp	olive oil	15 mL
3	cloves garlic, minced	3
2	onions, chopped	2
2	stalks celery, chopped	2
2 tsp	chili powder	10 mL
2 tsp	chopped fresh or pickled jalapeño pepper	10 mL
1-1/2 tsp	dried oregano	7 mL
1 tsp	ground cumin	5 mL
1/2 tsp	aniseed	2 mL
6 cups	vegetable stock	1.5 L
1	can (14 oz/398 mL) stewed tomatoes	1
3/4 tsp	salt	4 mL
1/4 tsp	pepper	1 mL
4 tsp	lime juice	20 mL

● Rinse beans, discarding any grit. In large pot, cover beans with three times their volume of water; bring to boil, cover and cook for 2 minutes. Remove from heat; let soak for 1 hour. Drain.

● Wipe out pot and heat oil over medium heat; cook garlic, onions and celery, stirring occasionally, for 5 minutes or until onions are softened. Add chili powder, jalapeño pepper, oregano, cumin and aniseed; cook, stirring occasionally, for 1 minute.

● Add beans and stock; bring to boil. Reduce heat, cover and simmer for 1 hour and 15 minutes or until beans are very tender. Add tomatoes, salt and pepper; simmer for 10 minutes.

● In food processor or blender, purée 8 cups (2 L) of the soup in batches. Return to pot; heat through. Stir in lime juice. *(Soup can be refrigerated in airtight container for up to 3 days or frozen for up to 2 months.)* Makes 6 servings.

QUICK-COOKING VARIATION
● Substitute three 19-oz (540 mL) cans of black beans, drained, for the soaked beans. Reduce stock to 5 cups (1.25 mL). To onion mixture, add beans, stock, tomatoes, salt and pepper; simmer for only 30 minutes.

B*e Prepared is a motto to remember when food shopping. It will remind you to stock up your pantry with black beans and tomatoes so you're ready for company — say, after an evening of skating.*

Per serving: about
- 410 calories
- 5 g fat
- good source of calcium
- very high source of fiber
- 26 g protein
- 69 g carbohydrate
- excellent source of iron

Two-Mushroom Barley Soup ▼

Dried mushrooms, especially porcini, are incredibly rich in woodsy essence. Only a few are needed to flavor a whole pot of soup.

Per serving: about
- 280 calories
- 11 g protein
- 7 g fat
- 46 g carbohydrate
- very high source of fiber
- excellent source of iron

1 oz	dried mushrooms (porcini or shiitake)	30 g
4	carrots	4
8 cups	button mushrooms (1 lb/500 g)	2 L
2 tbsp	vegetable oil	25 mL
2	onions, finely chopped	2
3	cloves garlic, minced	3
1-1/4 tsp	dried thyme	6 mL
3/4 tsp	crumbled dried sage	4 mL
1/2 tsp	pepper	2 mL
1/4 tsp	salt	1 mL
2 tbsp	tomato paste	25 mL
2 tbsp	soy sauce	25 mL
1 tbsp	balsamic or red wine vinegar	15 mL
1 cup	barley	250 mL
6 cups	vegetable stock	1.5 L
3 cups	water	750 mL
4 cups	packed fresh spinach	1 L

● Place dried mushrooms in small bowl; pour in 1 cup (250 mL) boiling water. Let stand for 20 minutes or until softened. Strain through cheesecloth-lined sieve, reserving liquid. (If using shiitakes, cut off tough stem end.) Slice mushrooms into thin strips; set aside.

● Meanwhile, peel and slice carrots diagonally. Trim and slice button mushrooms thickly.

● In large heavy saucepan, heat oil over medium heat; cook onions and garlic, stirring often, for 5 minutes or until softened. Add carrots and dried and button mushrooms; cook, stirring often, for 15 to 20 minutes or until mushrooms are lightly browned and liquid is evaporated.

● Stir in thyme, sage, pepper and salt. Stir in tomato paste, soy sauce, vinegar and reserved soaking liquid. Add barley; cook, stirring, for 1 to 2 minutes or until liquid is absorbed and barley is well coated.

● Add stock and water; bring to boil. Reduce heat, cover and simmer, stirring occasionally, for 50 minutes. Uncover and cook for 20 minutes or until slightly thickened. *(Soup can be prepared to this point and refrigerated in airtight container for up to 2 days; reheat gently, adding up to 1/2 cup/125 mL more water to thin if desired.)*

● Flatten spinach and stack leaves with stems all at one end. Roll up tightly; slice crosswise into 1/2-inch (1 cm) wide strips. Stir into soup; cover and cook for 3 minutes or until wilted. Makes 6 servings.

TIP: You can use a variety of fresh exotic mushrooms such as crimini, shiitake, portobello or oyster, if desired.

Lentil Rice Soup

2 tbsp	olive oil	25 mL
1	onion, chopped	1
2	cloves garlic, slivered	2
2	carrots, chopped	2
1-1/2 cups	green lentils	375 mL
1/2 cup	long-grain rice	125 mL
2 tbsp	paprika	25 mL
1 tsp	crumbled dried mint	5 mL
1/4 tsp	hot pepper flakes	1 mL
6 cups	vegetable stock (approx)	1.5 L
1	can (14 oz/398 mL) tomato sauce	1
1/3 cup	extra-thick plain yogurt	75 mL
1	lime or lemon, cut in wedges	1

● In large heavy saucepan, heat oil over medium-low heat; cook onion, garlic and carrots, stirring occasionally, for 5 minutes.

● Stir in lentils, rice, paprika, mint and hot pepper flakes; cook, stirring, for 5 minutes or until onion is softened and paprika has deepened in color.

● Pour in 6 cups (1.5 L) stock; bring to boil. Reduce heat, cover and simmer for 40 to 50 minutes or until lentils and rice are tender.

● Stir in tomato sauce; bring to simmer, adding more stock if thinner soup is desired. Ladle into bowls; garnish with yogurt. Serve with lime wedges to squeeze into soup. Makes 6 servings.

A squirt of fresh lime juice, a sprinkle of mint and a dollop of yogurt transform a workaday lentil-and-vegetable soup into a delightful treat!

Per serving: about
- 360 calories
- 8 g fat
- very high source of fiber
- 21 g protein
- 54 g carbohydrate
- excellent source of iron

TIP: When fresh mint is in season, use 2 tbsp (25 mL) chopped instead of dried and sprinkle extra on top of the soup just before serving.

Corn Chowder for Two

1 tsp	olive oil	5 mL
1	small onion, chopped	1
1	potato, peeled and diced	1
1	stalk celery, chopped	1
1/4 cup	diced sweet red pepper	50 mL
Pinch	hot pepper flakes	Pinch
1 cup	vegetable stock	250 mL
1/2 cup	1% milk	125 mL
1	can (10 oz/284 mL) creamed corn	1
1/4 cup	frozen corn kernels	50 mL
1/4 tsp	each salt and pepper	1 mL
1 tbsp	chopped fresh coriander, basil, thyme or parsley	15 mL

● In heavy saucepan, heat oil over medium heat; cook onion, potato, celery, red pepper and hot pepper flakes, stirring often, for 5 minutes.

● Pour in stock and bring to boil; reduce heat and simmer, covered, for 10 minutes or until potato is tender.

● Add milk, creamed corn, frozen corn, salt and pepper; heat gently until steaming. Ladle into bowls; sprinkle with coriander. Makes 2 servings.

Contrary to its name, creamed corn does not contain cream. Here, creamed corn adds a welcome smoothness to this medley of vegetables.

Per serving: about
- 270 calories
- 5 g fat
- high source of fiber
- 10 g protein
- 53 g carbohydrate

Broccoli Bean Soup

Nothing hits the spot on a chilly night like this full-flavored soup loaded with calcium-rich broccoli, beans, milk and cheese.

Per serving: about
- 225 calories
- 9 g fat
- high source of fiber
- 17 g protein
- 20 g carbohydrate
- excellent source of calcium

1 tbsp	vegetable oil	15 mL
1 cup	chopped onions	250 mL
2	cloves garlic, chopped	2
4 cups	coarsely chopped broccoli (about 1 bunch)	1 L
2-1/2 cups	vegetable stock	625 mL
1	potato, peeled and diced	1
1 cup	drained canned white pea (navy) beans	250 mL
1-1/2 cups	shredded light Cheddar-style cheese	375 mL
1 cup	1% milk	250 mL
1/4 tsp	each salt and pepper	1 mL

● In large heavy saucepan, heat oil over medium heat; cook onions and garlic, stirring occasionally, for about 5 minutes or until softened.

● Add broccoli, stock, potato and beans; bring to boil. Reduce heat, cover and simmer for about 20 minutes or until vegetables are softened.

● Transfer to food processor or blender; purée to desired consistency. Return to saucepan.

● Stir in half of the cheese, the milk, salt and pepper; cook over medium-low heat, stirring, just until cheese is melted. Ladle into bowls; sprinkle with remaining cheese. Makes 6 servings.

Hint-of-Spice Squash Soup

A vegetable such as squash adds its own creamy thickness to soup.

Per serving: about
- 125 calories
- 4 g fat
- 3 g protein
- 20 g carbohydrate

2 tbsp	vegetable oil	25 mL
2	onions, chopped	2
2	stalks celery, chopped	2
1	clove garlic, minced	1
2 tbsp	chopped fresh coriander or parsley	25 mL
1 tbsp	grated gingerroot	15 mL
1/2 tsp	each salt and pepper	2 mL
1/4 tsp	grated lime rind	1 mL
Pinch	chili powder	Pinch
8 cups	cubed peeled butternut or buttercup squash	2 L
2 cups	vegetable stock	500 mL
2 cups	water	500 mL
1 cup	low-fat plain yogurt	250 mL
	Fresh coriander sprigs	

● In large heavy saucepan, heat oil over medium heat; cook onions, celery, garlic, coriander, ginger, salt, pepper, lime rind and chili powder, stirring occasionally, for 8 to 10 minutes or until softened.

● Add squash, stock and water; bring to boil. Reduce heat, cover and simmer for about 20 minutes or until squash is tender.

● In blender or food processor, purée soup, in batches, until smooth. Reheat in clean saucepan over medium heat until steaming. Ladle into bowls. Swirl 2 tbsp (25 mL) yogurt into soup; garnish with coriander sprigs. Makes 8 servings.

Chick-Pea and Spinach Soup ▲

1 tbsp	olive oil	15 mL
4	cloves garlic, minced	4
2	onions, chopped	2
1	potato, peeled and cut in chunks	1
4 cups	vegetable stock	1 L
2 tbsp	each minced fresh parsley and coriander	25 mL
1 tsp	dried marjoram	5 mL
1	can (19 oz/540 mL) chick-peas, drained and rinsed	1
Half	pkg (10 oz/284 g) fresh spinach, trimmed and chopped	Half

● In large heavy saucepan, heat oil over medium-low heat; cook garlic and onions, stirring occasionally, for 5 minutes or until softened.

● Add potato; cook, stirring, for 1 minute. Add stock, parsley, coriander and marjoram; cover and simmer for 15 minutes or until potato is very tender. Stir in chick-peas.

● In food processor in batches or using hand blender in saucepan, purée just until chick-peas are coarse; return to pan. Add spinach; simmer for 5 minutes, adding 1/2 cup (125 mL) water if too thick. Makes 6 servings.

Mediterranean-inspired dishes such as this Portuguese soup get high marks for health. Other greens such as collards or Swiss chard can replace the spinach. The chick-peas are a rich source of fiber.

Per serving: about
- 155 calories
- 6 g protein
- 4 g fat
- 25 g carbohydrate
- high source of fiber

TIP: If desired, use 1 cup (250 mL) dried chick-peas to yield 2 cups (500 mL) cooked. Soak overnight. Drain and bring to boil in fresh water; reduce heat and simmer for 1 to 2 hours or until tender. Drain.

Hungarian Mushroom Soup

The recipe for this loaded-with-mushrooms soup comes from Dick Rendek, a Regina lawyer with a well-known fondness for fine food and football.

Per serving: about
- 215 calories
- 10 g protein
- 10 g fat
- 24 g carbohydrate
- good source of calcium and iron

2 tbsp	butter	25 mL
2 cups	chopped onions	500 mL
6 cups	sliced mushrooms (1 lb/500 g)	1.5 L
2 cups	vegetable stock	500 mL
1 tbsp	paprika (preferably Hungarian)	15 mL
1 tbsp	soy sauce	15 mL
1 tsp	dried dillweed	5 mL
3 tbsp	all-purpose flour	50 mL
1 cup	milk	250 mL
1 cup	water	250 mL
1/2 cup	light sour cream	125 mL
2 tsp	lemon juice	10 mL
1/2 tsp	pepper	2 mL
2 tbsp	chopped fresh parsley	25 mL

● In large heavy saucepan, heat butter over medium heat; cook onions, stirring occasionally, for 5 to 7 minutes or until softened.

● Add mushrooms, 1/2 cup (125 mL) of the stock, paprika, soy sauce and dillweed; cover and cook, stirring occasionally, for about 15 minutes or until mushrooms are softened.

● Sprinkle with flour; cook, stirring, for 30 seconds. Gradually stir in remaining stock, milk and water; cook, stirring, for 15 minutes or until thickened. Remove from heat. Stir in sour cream, lemon juice and pepper. Ladle into bowls; garnish with parsley. Makes 4 servings.

Quick Beet Borscht

When you want it quick and easy, use canned whole beets in this vivid soup. When time permits, simmer your own beets (see TIP, below).

Per serving: about
- 130 calories
- 4 g protein
- 1 g fat
- 27 g carbohydrate

2	cans (each 14 oz/ 398 mL) whole baby beets	2
2 cups	vegetable stock	500 mL
1	onion, chopped	1
1	stalk celery, sliced	1
1	potato, peeled and diced	1
1/2 tsp	dried dillweed (or 1 tbsp/15 mL chopped fresh dill)	2 mL
1/2 cup	finely shredded cabbage	125 mL
2 tsp	cider vinegar	10 mL
1/4 cup	light sour cream or thick plain yogurt	50 mL
2 tbsp	sliced green onion tops	25 mL

● Drain beets, reserving liquid in large saucepan; cube beets and set aside.

● Add stock to pan; bring to boil. Add onion, celery, potato and dillweed; return to boil. Reduce heat, cover and simmer for 15 minutes or until vegetables are tender.

● Add cabbage; cook, covered, for about 5 minutes or until tender-crisp. Add beets and vinegar; heat through. Ladle into bowls. Swirl in sour cream; sprinkle with green onion. Makes 4 servings.

TIP: To replace the canned beets with fresh cooked, scrub and trim 8 beets (2 lb/1 kg). Cook in boiling water for about 40 minutes or until skins slip off easily. Drain, reserving 1-1/2 cups (375 mL) cooking liquid. Let beets cool; skin and cube.

Minestrone with Sun-Dried Tomato Pesto

3/4 cup	dried white beans (Great Northern or pea beans)	175 mL
1 tbsp	olive oil	15 mL
1	large onion, chopped	1
1	leek (white and light green part only), chopped	1
2	cloves garlic, minced	2
2	carrots, chopped	2
2	stalks celery, chopped	2
10 cups	vegetable stock	2.5 L
2 cups	shredded cabbage	500 mL
2 cups	small cauliflower florets	500 mL
1/3 cup	short fine egg noodles or other small pasta shape	75 mL
1 cup	frozen peas	250 mL
	Tomato Pesto (recipe follows)	
	Freshly grated Parmesan cheese (optional)	

● Sort and rinse beans. In large saucepan, bring beans and 6 cups (1.5 L) cold water to boil; reduce heat and simmer for 2 minutes. Let stand for 1 hour; drain and return to pot. Add 8 cups (2 L) cold water; bring to boil over high heat. Reduce heat and simmer, partially covered, for 1 hour or until tender. Drain.

● Meanwhile, in stockpot or 32-cup (8 L) Dutch oven, heat oil over medium heat; cook onion, leek, garlic, carrots and celery, stirring often, for 10 minutes or until softened.

● Add stock and cabbage; bring to boil over high heat. Reduce heat, cover and simmer for 20 minutes or just until vegetables are tender. Stir in cauliflower and pasta; simmer, covered, for 8 minutes or until pasta is tender. Stir in peas and beans; cook for 2 minutes. *(Can be refrigerated in airtight container for up to 5 days or frozen for up to 1 month. Add more stock when reheating if necessary.)*

● Ladle into bowls; swirl generous tablespoonful (15 mL) tomato pesto into each. Sprinkle with Parmesan cheese (if using). Makes 10 servings.

TOMATO PESTO

1/2 cup	sun-dried dry-packed tomatoes	125 mL
1/2 cup	packed fresh basil leaves	125 mL
1/2 cup	packed fresh parsley sprigs	125 mL
1	large clove garlic	1
1/3 cup	vegetable stock	75 mL
2 tbsp	olive oil	25 mL
1/3 cup	freshly grated Parmesan cheese	75 mL
1/2 tsp	pepper	2 mL

● In bowl, cover tomatoes with boiling water; let stand for 10 minutes or until softened. Drain and pat dry; chop coarsely.

● In food processor, chop together tomatoes, basil, parsley and garlic; with motor running, gradually pour in stock and oil in thin stream. Stir in Parmesan cheese and pepper. *(Pesto can be refrigerated in airtight container for up to 5 days or frozen for up to 1 month.)* Makes 3/4 cup (175 mL).

Per 1 tbsp (15 mL): about
• 45 calories • 2 g protein • 3 g fat • 2 g carbohydrate

T*he pesto adds wonderful flavor to this hearty main-course soup. Any combination of vegetables can be used, depending on what's in the fridge.*

For each of 10 servings: about
• 175 calories
• 6 g fat
• high source of fiber
• 8 g protein
• 22 g carbohydrate

TIPS

● Instead of soaking and precooking dried beans, you can use 1 can (19 oz/540 mL) navy or romano beans, drained and rinsed.

● If fresh basil is unavailable, increase parsley to 1 cup (250 mL) and add 1 tbsp (15 mL) dried basil.

Salads, Sandwiches and Pizzas

Add spark to weekly menus with this trio of new standbys — main-dish salads, hearty sandwiches and pizza pleasers. Vegetarian dishes have never tasted so good or been so easy to make.

Harvest Stuffed Tomatoes ▶

Cup a colorful, crunchy salad in sun-drenched beefsteak tomatoes. Tomato juice replaces some of the oil in the dressing, making it lower in fat than usual.

Per serving: about
- 170 calories
- 4 g protein
- 9 g fat
- 23 g carbohydrate
- high source of fiber

1	onion	1
1 tsp	olive oil	5 mL
1	clove garlic, minced	1
1 cup	corn kernels	250 mL
1	zucchini, diced	1
1	sweet red pepper, diced	1
2 tbsp	tomato juice	25 mL
1/4 tsp	each salt and pepper	1 mL
4	beefsteak tomatoes	4
	VINAIGRETTE	
2 tbsp	white wine vinegar	25 mL
2 tbsp	tomato juice	25 mL
2 tbsp	olive oil	25 mL

1 tsp	chopped fresh thyme (or 1/4 tsp/1 mL dried)	5 mL
1/2 tsp	Dijon mustard	2 mL
Pinch	granulated sugar	Pinch

● Cut onion in half crosswise; thinly slice lengthwise. In nonstick skillet, heat oil over medium heat; cook onion and garlic, stirring often, for about 7 minutes or until softened.

● Stir in corn, zucchini, red pepper, tomato juice, salt and pepper; cook, stirring often, for 10 minutes or until vegetables are tender and liquid is absorbed. Remove from heat.

● VINAIGRETTE: Whisk together vinegar, tomato juice, oil, thyme, mustard and sugar; pour over vegetables.

● Slice tomatoes into wedges, without cutting through to bottom; fan out to resemble flowers. Spoon vegetable mixture into tomatoes. Makes 4 servings.

THE BEST BREADS

Even though all Canadian baked goods are made with enriched flour, the best choice when buying a loaf, rolls or flatbread are products made with whole grains; they have the most nutrients, flavor, fiber and texture. Whole wheat, seven grain, muesli, flax, bran and oatmeal breads are examples that have traditionally offered more than plain white. However, some breads are now being enhanced with protein, calcium and additional fiber to make the bread not only more enjoyable, but more healthful than ever.

Cauliflower Lemon Salad ◄

1	head cauliflower, cut in florets	1
1	small lemon, thinly sliced	1
2 cups	cherry tomatoes, halved	500 mL
1 cup	olives	250 mL
1/2 cup	extra-virgin olive oil	125 mL
1/4 cup	white vinegar	50 mL
2 tbsp	chopped fresh parsley	25 mL
	Juice of 1 lemon	
2 tsp	minced fresh oregano (or 1 tsp/5 mL dried)	10 mL
1 tsp	dry mustard	5 mL
1	clove garlic, minced	1
Pinch	each salt and pepper	Pinch
	Fresh oregano leaves	

● In bowl, pour boiling water over cauliflower and lemon slices; let stand for 8 minutes. Drain well and place in salad bowl along with tomatoes and olives.

● In jar with tight-fitting lid, shake together oil, vinegar, parsley, lemon juice, oregano, mustard, garlic, salt and pepper; pour over vegetables and toss well to combine. Cover and refrigerate for 2 hours before serving with slotted spoon. *(Salad can be refrigerated in airtight container for up to 2 days.)* Serve garnished with oregano leaves. Makes 6 servings.

*S*alty dark-green olives, crisp cauliflower and tangy sun-ripened tomatoes bring contrasting flavors, textures and colors to a simple yet sophisticated year-round salad.

Per serving: about
- 225 calories
- 2 g protein
- 21 g fat
- 10 g carbohydrate

TIP: Look for the more flavorful flat-leaf (Italian) parsley.

Artichoke Salad

2	cans (14 oz/398 mL each) artichoke hearts	2
3	sweet green peppers	3
1	sweet red pepper	1
2	tomatoes	2
3 tbsp	olive oil	50 mL
3 tbsp	red wine vinegar	50 mL
1 tsp	Dijon mustard	5 mL
1	clove garlic, minced	1
1/4 tsp	each salt and pepper	1 mL
8	green olives, pitted	8
	Lettuce leaves	
3	hard-cooked eggs, cut in wedges	3

● Drain artichoke hearts; cut into quarters. Seed, core and cut green and red peppers into 1-inch (2.5 cm) squares. Chop tomatoes.

● In 8-cup (2 L) container with tight-fitting lid, whisk together oil, vinegar, mustard, garlic, salt and pepper. Layer one-third each of the artichokes, green and red peppers, tomatoes and olives. Repeat layers twice.

● Seal and turn container upside down. Marinate at room temperature for 2 hours, turning upside down every 30 minutes.

● To serve, arrange on lettuce-lined plates; garnish with eggs. Makes 4 servings.

*S*upper dish or lunch entrée, take your pick with this chunky egg and-vegetable dish that's at its best when summer produce is at its peak.

Per serving: about
- 275 calories
- 11 g protein
- 17 g fat
- 26 g carbohydrate
- very high source of fiber
- good source of iron

Antipasto Salad ▶

With frisky vinaigrettes, salads are one of the best ways to integrate the rather bland tofu into menus. Crusty bread is a must with the salad.

Per serving: about
- 270 calories
- 16 g fat
- high source of fiber
- 13 g protein
- 21 g carbohydrate
- good source of calcium

4 oz	extra-firm tofu	125 g
1 cup	broccoli florets	250 mL
1	can (19 oz/540 mL) chick-peas	1
1	small sweet red or green pepper	1
Half	seedless cucumber	Half
1 cup	halved cherry tomatoes	250 mL
1/4 cup	black olives (preferably Kalamata)	50 mL
3 oz	mozzarella cheese, cubed (1/2 cup/125 mL)	75 g
2 tbsp	chopped fresh parsley	25 mL
2 oz	feta cheese, crumbled	50 g
	DRESSING	
2 tbsp	red wine vinegar	25 mL
1	green onion, minced	1
2	cloves garlic, minced	2
1 tsp	Dijon mustard	5 mL
1/2 tsp	each dried basil and oregano	2 mL
1/4 tsp	each salt and pepper	1 mL
3 tbsp	olive oil	50 mL

● DRESSING: In bowl, whisk together vinegar, onion, garlic, mustard, basil, oregano, salt and pepper; gradually whisk in oil.

● Cut tofu into 1-1/2-inch (4 cm) long strips, about 1/4 inch (5 mm) wide; add to dressing. Let stand at room temperature for 1 hour.

● In saucepan of boiling salted water, cook broccoli just until tender-crisp; drain and refresh under cold water. Drain again; place in large bowl. Rinse chick-peas under cold water; drain and add to bowl.

● Slice red pepper into thin strips and cucumber into chunks; add to bowl along with tomatoes, olives, mozzarella cheese and parsley. Add tofu and dressing; toss gently. Cover and refrigerate, stirring occasionally, for at least 1 hour or until chilled. *(Salad can be refrigerated in airtight container for up to 2 days.)* Toss gently and serve sprinkled with feta cheese. Makes 6 servings.

Pasta Garden Salad

Add a crusty whole wheat loaf and a frosty pitcher of lemonade, then head out to the deck with this summer salad that's abundant with fresh herbs.

Per serving: about
- 315 calories
- 9 g fat
- very high source of fiber
- 12 g protein
- 48 g carbohydrate
- good source of iron

2 cups	rotini pasta	500 mL
1	zucchini	1
1	large tomato, chopped	1
2 cups	sliced mushrooms (about 6 oz/175 g)	500 mL
1/4 cup	chopped red onion	50 mL
1	can (19 oz/540 mL) chick-peas or black or red kidney beans, drained and rinsed	1
	HERB SALAD DRESSING	
3 tbsp	water	50 mL
2 tbsp	extra-virgin olive oil	25 mL
2 tbsp	balsamic vinegar	25 mL
2 tbsp	lemon juice	25 mL
1	clove garlic, minced	1
1/2 tsp	each salt and pepper	2 mL
1/4 cup	chopped fresh basil	50 mL
1 tbsp	chopped fresh oregano	15 mL

● In saucepan of boiling salted water, cook rotini for about 8 minutes or until tender but firm; drain well.

● HERB SALAD DRESSING: Meanwhile, in large bowl, whisk together water, oil, vinegar, lemon juice, garlic, salt and pepper; stir in basil and oregano.

● Cut zucchini lengthwise into quarters; cut crosswise into slices and add to bowl with tomato, mushrooms, onion and chick-peas. Add rotini; toss to combine. Makes 4 servings.

Mexican Quesadilla Salad

For a sophisticated repast, top a warmed flour tortilla with a toss of romaine, tomatoes and chick-peas, then dollop with a zesty avocado dressing.

Per serving: about
- 620 calories
- 27 g protein
- 28 g fat
- 68 g carbohydrate
- very high source of fiber
- excellent source of calcium and iron

Half	small red onion, sliced	Half
1	head romaine lettuce	1
3	large tomatoes, diced	3
1	can (19 oz/540 mL) chick-peas, drained and rinsed	1
1-1/3 cups	shredded Cheddar cheese	325 mL
4	8-inch (20 cm) flour tortillas	4
1/4 cup	chopped fresh coriander (optional)	50 mL
	AVOCADO DRESSING	
3/4 cup	plain low-fat yogurt	175 mL
1	large avocado, peeled and pitted	1
1/4 cup	chopped green onions	50 mL
2 tbsp	lime juice	25 mL
1	fresh red chili pepper, coarsely chopped	1
1/4 tsp	each salt and pepper	1 mL

● Soak onion in bowl of ice water for 15 minutes; drain well. Separate head of romaine and tear into bite-size pieces. In bowl, toss together onion, romaine, tomatoes, chick-peas and Cheddar cheese.

● AVOCADO DRESSING: In blender or food processor, purée yogurt, avocado, green onions, lime juice, red chili pepper, salt and pepper until smooth and creamy. Pour over salad; toss to coat well.

● In nonstick skillet, warm tortillas over medium-high heat for 30 seconds on each side or until lightly toasted. Lay tortilla on each plate; arrange salad over top. Sprinkle with coriander (if using). Makes 4 servings.

Spicy Bean Enchiladas

Here's a nifty recipe for first-time cooks to try. Guaranteed — everyone will enjoy the results!

Per serving: about
- 430 calories
- 18 g protein
- 13 g fat
- 64 g carbohydrate
- very high source of fiber
- good source of calcium
- excellent source of iron

1 tbsp	vegetable oil	15 mL
1	each onion and sweet green pepper, chopped	1
3	cloves garlic, minced	3
1 tbsp	each ground cumin and chili powder	15 mL
2 tsp	dried oregano	10 mL
Pinch	hot pepper flakes	Pinch
1	can (19 oz/540 mL) kidney beans, drained and rinsed	1
1 cup	salsa	250 mL
4	10-inch (25 cm) flour tortillas	4
1/2 cup	shredded Cheddar cheese	125 mL

● In nonstick skillet, heat oil over medium-high heat; cook onion and green pepper, stirring often, for 8 minutes or until softened.

● Stir in garlic, cumin, chili powder, oregano and hot pepper flakes; cook, stirring, for 2 minutes. Add beans and mash coarsely. *(Recipe can be prepared to this point and refrigerated in airtight container for up to 1 day.)* Stir in half of the salsa; cook, stirring, often, for 8 minutes.

● Divide mixture among tortillas and roll up. Place tortillas, seam side down, in lightly greased 11- x 7-inch (2 L) glass baking dish. Spoon remaining salsa over top; sprinkle with Cheddar cheese. Cover with foil; bake in 450°F (230°C) oven for 10 minutes. Or cover with waxed paper and microwave at High for 5 minutes. Makes 4 servings.

Grilled Eggplant Sandwiches ▲

1	eggplant (about 1 lb/500 g)	1
1 tbsp	olive oil	15 mL
1/4 tsp	each salt and pepper	1 mL
3 oz	fontina cheese, thinly sliced	90 g
16	fresh basil leaves	16

● Cut eggplant crosswise into 1/2-inch (1 cm) thick slices. Brush each side with oil; sprinkle with salt and pepper.

● Place on greased grill over medium-high heat; close lid and cook for 8 minutes. Turn eggplant; top half of the slices with cheese. Cook, covered, for about 7 minutes or until eggplant is softened and cheese is melted.

● Dividing evenly, place basil leaves on cheese; top with remaining plain slices of eggplant. Makes 4 servings.

Slices of eggplant substitute for bread in this tasty new take on a supper sandwich. For even greater eating pleasure, add slices of roasted sweet red pepper or even fresh arugula leaves instead of the basil.

Per serving: about
- 145 calories
- 6 g protein
- 10 g fat
- 8 g carbohydrate

Herbed French Toast Sandwiches ▶

We married good old grilled cheese sandwiches (only made with Dijon mustard and melty Fontina cheese) and cozy French toast. The result — a flavor sensation.

Per serving: about
- 445 calories
- 21 g protein
- 17 g fat
- 51 g carbohydrate
- good source of calcium and iron

4	eggs	4
2/3 cup	milk	150 mL
1 tsp	dried basil	5 mL
1/4 tsp	pepper	1 mL
Pinch	salt	Pinch
8	slices (3/4-inch/2 cm thick) Italian bread	8
1 tbsp	Dijon mustard	15 mL
4 oz	Fontina or Swiss cheese, thinly sliced	125 g
2 tsp	butter	10 mL
1/4 cup	red pepper jelly	50 mL

● In large shallow dish, whisk together eggs, milk, basil, pepper and salt; set aside.

● Spread 4 of the bread slices with mustard; top with cheese slices, then remaining bread. Dip sandwiches into egg mixture, turning to soak through and use up all the egg.

● In large nonstick skillet or electric griddle, melt butter over medium heat; cook sandwiches, turning once, for 3 minutes on each side or until brown and cheese is melted. Serve with red pepper jelly. Makes 4 servings.

Skinny Omelette Roll-Up for One

The ultimate quick supper — just an egg, a tortilla, a bit of cheese, a nonstick skillet and you!

Per serving: about
- 220 calories
- 11 g protein
- 10 g fat
- 20 g carbohydrate

1	egg	1
1 tbsp	milk	15 mL
Pinch	each salt and pepper	Pinch
1/4 tsp	vegetable oil	1 mL
1	7-inch (18 cm) flour tortilla	1
1 tbsp	shredded brick cheese	15 mL
1 tsp	chopped fresh parsley (optional)	5 mL

● Whisk together egg, milk, salt and pepper. Heat 6-inch (15 cm) nonstick skillet over medium-high heat; brush with oil. Pour in egg mixture, tilting to spread evenly; cook, piercing any bubbles, for about 1 minute or until set. Slide onto tortilla; sprinkle with cheese, and parsley (if using). Roll up. Makes 1 serving.

TIP: Try any combination of herbs and cheese, such as Cheddar and chives, or mozzarella and basil.

Tortilla Tofu Roll-Ups

Make-ahead cold-sandwich suppers are handy for warm weather. Add a bountiful salad, or serve with light soup.

Per serving: about
- 265 calories
- 10 g protein
- 7 g fat
- 43 g carbohydrate
- excellent source of iron

8 oz	silken firm tofu	250 g
1/2 cup	salsa	125 mL
1	sweet red pepper, chopped	1
1/4 cup	pitted black olives	50 mL
1 tsp	grated lime rind	5 mL
2 tbsp	lime juice	25 mL
8	6-inch (15 cm) flour tortillas	8
1/4 cup	chopped fresh coriander	50 mL

● In food processor, purée together tofu, salsa, half of the red pepper, the olives, and lime rind and juice until smooth. Spread 1/4 cup (50 mL) onto each tortilla, leaving 1/2-inch (1 cm) border. Sprinkle evenly with remaining red pepper and coriander.

● Roll up and wrap in plastic wrap. Refrigerate for 1 hour. *(Rolls can be refrigerated for up to 12 hours.)* Makes 4 servings.

Tortilla Egg Cups ▲

D*on't forget how delicious, inexpensive and nutritious eggs can be for suppers or weekend breakfasts and brunches. Tortillas give them a new twist and baking makes them easier to serve to a bunch.*

Per serving: about
- 180 calories
- 9 g protein
- 7 g fat
- 20 g carbohydrate

6	6-inch (20 cm) flour or corn tortillas	6
Half	each sweet red and green pepper, finely chopped	Half
2 tbsp	chopped fresh coriander or parsley	25 mL
2 tsp	minced jalapeño pepper	10 mL
6	eggs	6
Pinch	each salt and pepper	Pinch

● Lightly grease 6 deep muffin cups. Gently press tortilla into each, making three pleats to fit cup.

● Mix together red and green peppers, coriander and jalapeño pepper. Reserving 1/4 cup (50 mL), spoon remaining pepper mixture into tortillas. Break 1 egg on top of each, being careful not to break yolks. Sprinkle with salt and pepper.

● Bake in 375°F (190°C) oven for about 20 minutes or until whites are set and yolks are still runny. Serve sprinkled with remaining pepper mixture. Makes 6 servings.

Lentil and Bean Burgers

1/2 cup	dried brown lentils	125 mL
1 cup	rinsed drained canned red kidney beans	250 mL
2/3 cup	wheat germ	150 mL
1/3 cup	finely chopped pecans	75 mL
1 tbsp	butter	15 mL
3-1/2 cups	finely chopped mushrooms (about 8 oz/250 g)	825 mL
1	onion, chopped	1
1	clove garlic, minced	1
1/2 tsp	each ground cumin, salt and pepper	2 mL
1/4 cup	chili sauce	50 mL
4	sesame seed hamburger buns	4

● Sort lentils, discarding any discolored ones; rinse and drain. In saucepan, cover lentils with salted water; bring to boil. Reduce heat to low; cover and cook for 25 to 45 minutes or until tender. Drain and transfer to food processor. Add kidney beans; purée until smooth. Transfer to large bowl; set aside.

● In large nonstick skillet, toast wheat germ and pecans over medium-high heat for about 2 minutes or until wheat germ is golden and fragrant; add to lentil mixture.

● Add butter to skillet; cook mushrooms, onion, garlic, cumin, salt and pepper, stirring occasionally, for about 15 minutes or until mushrooms are softened and moisture is evaporated. Let cool slightly; add to bowl. Add chili sauce; mix thoroughly. Form into four 3/4-inch (2 cm)) thick patties.

● Place patties on greased grill over medium-high heat or on greased baking sheet under broiler; close lid and cook, turning once, for 10 to 12 minutes or until golden brown and crisp. Sandwich in buns. Makes 4 servings.

TIP: The dried lentils can be replaced with 1-1/3 cups (325 mL) drained and rinsed canned lentils; just omit the cooking in the water. Use the extra lentils from the can to add to a salad or soup.

It's handy to have a good recipe for vegetarian burgers — especially in the summer, when the barbecue is king.

Per serving: about
- 510 calories
- 16 g fat
- very high source of fiber
- 22 g protein
- 76 g carbohydrate
- excellent source of iron

Rice and Tofu Burgers

2 tsp	vegetable oil	10 mL
2	cloves garlic, minced	2
1	small onion, chopped	1
2 tsp	chili powder	10 mL
1/4 tsp	salt	1 mL
1/2 cup	short-grain rice	125 mL
1-1/4 cups	vegetable stock or water	300 mL
6 oz	extra-firm tofu, drained	175 g
1	carrot	1
1/4 cup	quick-cooking rolled oats	50 mL

● In saucepan, heat oil over medium heat; cook garlic, onion, chili powder and salt, stirring occasionally, for about 5 minutes or until softened.

● Stir in rice, then stock. Bring to boil; reduce heat, cover and simmer for about 20 minutes or until rice is tender and liquid is absorbed. Transfer to bowl; let cool.

● Meanwhile, coarsely grate tofu and carrot. With potato masher or fork, mash rice mixture slightly; mix in tofu, carrot and rolled oats. Shape into four 1/2-inch (1 cm) thick patties. *(Patties can be wrapped in plastic wrap and refrigerated for up to 24 hours.)*

● Place patties on greased grill over medium-high heat or on greased baking sheet; close lid and cook, turning once, for 10 to 12 minutes on grill, 14 minutes under broiler, or until crispy outside. Makes 4 servings.

Burgers done over glowing coals are the perfect summer fare to pop into toasted rolls and top with tomatoes, onions, sprouts for crunch and whatever else that tickles your fancy.

Per serving: about
- 200 calories
- 4 g fat
- 10 g protein
- 31 g carbohydrate

Spinach Ricotta Loaf

A round ring loaf stuffed with spinach, mild ricotta cheese and eggs is impressive for any meal of the day, but especially suitable for weekend brunch, lunch or supper.

Per serving: about
- 180 calories
- 12 g protein
- 6 g fat
- 18 g carbohydrate
- good source of calcium and iron

1	ring (12-inch/30 cm) Italian bread (1 lb/500 g)	1
2 tsp	olive oil	10 mL
4-1/2 cups	sliced mushrooms (about 12 oz/375 g)	1.125 L
3	cloves garlic, minced	3
1-1/2 tsp	dried basil	7 mL
3/4 tsp	salt	4 mL
1/2 tsp	pepper	2 mL
3 cups	packed fresh spinach, trimmed and chopped	750 mL
1/3 cup	chopped green onions	75 mL
Half	sweet red pepper, chopped	Half
1	tub (475 g) light ricotta cheese (about 2 cups/500 mL)	1
1/3 cup	freshly grated Parmesan cheese	75 mL
6	eggs	6

● Slice bread in half horizontally; hollow out rings, leaving 1-inch (2.5 cm) thick crust. Reserve bread crumbs for another use.

● In nonstick skillet, heat oil over medium-high heat; cook mushrooms, garlic, basil, salt and pepper, stirring occasionally, for 8 minutes or until browned and liquid is evaporated. Stir in spinach, onions and red pepper; cook for 2 minutes or until spinach is wilted and liquid is evaporated.

● In bowl, whisk together ricotta and Parmesan cheeses and eggs; stir in mushroom mixture. Mound into bottom half of loaf; top with other half. Wrap loosely in foil. Bake in 400°F (200°C) oven for 50 minutes. Let stand for 10 minutes. Serve in thick slices. Makes 12 servings.

Cheesy Bean Quesadillas

Get a head start on supper by preparing the bean mixture a few hours before you plan to assemble these vegetable-rich baked quesadillas.

Per serving: about
- 450 calories
- 24 g protein
- 10 g fat
- 68 g carbohydrate
- very high source of fiber
- excellent source of calcium and iron

1	small jalapeño pepper	1
1	can (19 oz/540 mL) pinto or red kidney beans, drained and rinsed	1
1/4 cup	salsa	50 mL
2 tbsp	chopped red onion	25 mL
1 tsp	chili powder	5 mL
1/2 tsp	each ground cumin and dried oregano	2 mL
1/2 tsp	salt	2 mL
8	8-inch (20 cm) soft flour tortillas	8
1 cup	shredded light Monterey Jack-style cheese (4 oz/125 g)	250 mL
1/2 cup	each frozen corn kernels and peas	125 mL
1/4 cup	plain low-fat yogurt	50 mL

● Seed jalapeño pepper. In food processor, chop pepper. Add kidney beans, salsa, 2 tbsp (25 mL) water, onion, chili powder, cumin, oregano and salt; chop just until chunky. *(Bean mixture can be refrigerated in airtight container for up to 24 hours.)*

● Lay 4 tortillas on work surface; spread with bean mixture. Sprinkle with cheese, corn and peas. Spread remaining tortillas with yogurt; invert onto filling. Place on baking sheets; bake in 400°F (200°C) oven for 10 minutes or until golden and cheese is melted. Makes 4 servings.

TIP: Always protect your hands with rubber gloves when handling hot peppers such as jalapeños.

Hummus Wraps

6	7-inch (18 cm) tortillas	6
1/2 cup	each chopped cucumber, tomato and green onion	125 mL
1/3 cup	alfalfa or bean sprouts	75 mL
	HUMMUS	
1/4 cup	lightly packed fresh parsley	50 mL
1	can (19 oz/540 mL) chick-peas, drained and rinsed	1
1/4 cup	tahini	50 mL
3 tbsp	lemon juice	50 mL
2 tbsp	toasted sesame seeds	25 mL
2 tbsp	water	25 mL
1 tbsp	vegetable oil	15 mL
1/2 tsp	each salt, ground cumin and coriander	2 mL
1/4 tsp	pepper	1 mL
1	clove garlic, minced	1

● HUMMUS: In food processor, chop parsley and chick-peas finely. Add tahini, lemon juice, sesame seeds, water, oil, salt, cumin, coriander and pepper; purée until smooth. Mix in garlic. *(Hummus can be refrigerated in airtight container for up to 3 days.)*

● Spread 1/3 cup (75 mL) hummus over each tortilla; sprinkle cucumber, tomato and green onion evenly over each. Sprinkle each with about 1 tbsp (15 mL) alfalfa sprouts.

● Fold bottom of tortilla up about 1 inch (2.5 cm); roll one side tightly into center, then roll other side into center. Wrap each bundle tightly in plastic wrap. Makes 6 servings.

For a no-mess, easy-to-hold package, try this totally satisfying sandwich. For variety, roll the tortillas and hummus around grilled peppers and eggplant. What a refreshing change of taste!

Per serving: about
- 325 calories
- 13 g fat
- high source of fiber
- 11 g protein
- 44 g carbohydrate
- excellent source of iron

TIPS

● Tahini, a thick paste made of ground sesame seeds, is available in Middle Eastern grocery stores and some supermarkets.

● To toast sesame seeds, cook in skillet over medium heat, shaking pan occasionally, for about 5 minutes or until seeds are fragrant and golden.

Tex-Mex Corn Pizza

1	12-inch (30 cm) prebaked pizza crust	1
4 tsp	Dijon mustard	20 mL
1-1/4 cups	shredded light Monterey Jack-style cheese (about 5 oz/150 g)	300 mL
2 cups	cooked corn kernels	500 mL
3	green onions, chopped	3
1/4 cup	chopped fresh coriander or parsley	50 mL
2 tbsp	chopped canned green chilies or pickled jalapeño peppers	25 mL
1	large tomato, sliced	1
1	sweet green pepper, cut in rings	1

● Place pizza crust on perforated pizza pan or baking sheet. Brush with mustard. Sprinkle with 1/2 cup (125 mL) of the cheese. In bowl, toss together corn, green onions, coriander and chilies.

● Arrange tomato slices in single layer over crust, overlapping slightly; repeat with green pepper. Spoon corn mixture evenly over top. Sprinkle with remaining cheese. Bake in bottom third of 425°F (220°C) oven for 12 to 15 minutes or until crust is crisp and cheese is melted. Makes 4 servings.

A prebaked pizza and a healthful assortment of vegetables make this no-fuss Tex-Mex pizza a winner on all counts.

Per serving: about
- 380 calories
- 10 g fat
- high source of fiber
- good source of iron
- 19 g protein
- 56 g carbohydrate
- excellent source of calcium

Pronto Personal Pizzas ▼

*P*izzas are the perfect
showcase for fresh, ripe
tomatoes. This versatile
recipe allows you to make the
herbed dough in the food
processor or by hand, and to
cook the pizzas to puffed
crustiness either in the oven
or on the barbecue.

Per pizza: about
- 425 calories
- 16 g protein
- 11 g fat
- 66 g carbohydrate
- high source of fiber
- good source of calcium
- excellent source of iron

4-1/2 cups	all-purpose flour (approx)	1.125 L
2	pkg quick-rising (instant) dry yeast (or 2 tbsp/25 mL)	2
1/4 cup	finely chopped fresh basil	50 mL
2 tsp	salt	10 mL
1 tsp	granulated sugar	5 mL
1 tbsp	olive oil	15 mL
1/2 cup	cornmeal	125 mL
	TOPPING	
1 cup	shredded mozzarella cheese	250 mL
7	small tomatoes, sliced	7
1	small zucchini, thinly sliced	1
Quarter	small red onion, cut in thin wedges	Quarter
1 cup	yellow cherry tomatoes, halved (or 1 sweet yellow pepper, julienned)	250 mL
1 cup	shredded Asiago or provolone cheese	250 mL
1/3 cup	shredded fresh basil	75 mL

● In bowl, combine 4 cups (1 L) of the flour, yeast, basil, salt and sugar. Stir in 1-3/4 cups (425 mL) very hot water (120° to 130°F/50° to 55°C) and oil. Beat in enough of the remaining flour to make firm but soft dough. Turn out onto lightly floured surface; knead for 10 minutes or until smooth and elastic. Cover and let stand for 15 minutes.

● Dust 3 rimmed baking sheets with cornmeal. Divide dough into 8 pieces. On lightly floured surface, roll out or pat each into 6-inch (15 cm) circle. Press all over to form slightly raised rim. Transfer to sheets.

● TOPPING: Evenly sprinkle mozzarella cheese over each circle of dough. Arrange tomatoes and zucchini on top, overlapping slices. Top with onion and yellow cherry tomatoes. Sprinkle with Asiago cheese. Let stand for 15 minutes. (For a plumper crust, let stand for 30 to 40 minutes.)

● Bake in 450°F (230°C) oven, one pan at a time, for 10 to 15 minutes or until bottoms are crisp and cheese is melted. Sprinkle with shredded basil. Makes 8 pizzas.

VARIATION
● BARBECUED PRONTO PERSONAL PIZZAS: Omit cornmeal; lightly grease baking sheets. To cook, place pans on grill over medium-high heat; close lid and cook for 12 minutes or until bottoms are crisp and cheese is melted.

TIP: To make dough in food processor, combine 4-1/4 cups (1.05 L) of the flour, yeast, basil, salt and sugar. With motor running, gradually pour in 1-1/2 cups (375 mL) very hot water; add oil. Whirl, adding up to 2 tbsp (25 mL) more water, if necessary, until ball forms. Continue for 1 minute. Turn out onto floured surface; cover and let stand for 15 minutes.

Scrambled Egg Pizza Melts ▲

2	English muffins, split	2
1/4 cup	tomato sauce	50 mL
1 tbsp	butter	15 mL
1/2 cup	sliced mushrooms	125 mL
1/3 cup	chopped sweet green pepper	75 mL
4	eggs	4
2 tbsp	milk	25 mL
Pinch	each salt and pepper	Pinch
1/4 cup	shredded mozzarella cheese	50 mL

● Under broiler or in toaster oven, toast English muffins for about 1 minute or until golden. Spread each with 1 tbsp (15 mL) tomato sauce; set aside.

● Meanwhile, in nonstick skillet, melt butter over medium heat; cook mushrooms and green pepper, stirring occasionally, for about 5 minutes or until softened.

● Whisk together eggs, milk, salt and pepper; add to pan and cook, stirring, for about 1 minute or until softly set. Spoon over muffins. Sprinkle with mozzarella cheese; broil for about 1 minute or until melted. Makes 4 servings.

J oin two winners — scrambled eggs and pizza — for a lightning-quick entrée.

Per serving: about
- 220 calories
- 11 g fat
- 11 g protein
- 18 g carbohydrate

TIP: For more of a pizza taste, add a pinch of dried oregano to the egg mixture.

Grilled-Vegetable Pizza ◀

1	small eggplant	1
1	zucchini	1
2 tbsp	olive oil	25 mL
1	12-inch (30 cm) prebaked pizza crust	1
1/4 cup	pesto	50 mL
1 tbsp	chopped fresh oregano (or 1 tbsp/5 mL dried)	15 mL
1/4 cup	sliced red onion	50 mL
1 cup	shredded part-skim mozzarella cheese	250 mL

● Slice eggplant crosswise and zucchini lengthwise into 1/4-inch (5 mm) thick slices; brush with oil. Place on greased grill over medium-high heat; close lid and cook, turning once, for about 5 minutes or until well marked and tender.

● Place pizza crust on pizza pan or baking sheet; spread with pesto. Arrange eggplant and zucchini over top; sprinkle with oregano. Arrange red onion over top; sprinkle with mozzarella cheese.

● Bake in 500°F (260°C) oven for 8 to 10 minutes, or on grill for about 12 minutes, or until crust is crisp and cheese is melted and bubbly. Makes 4 servings.

Pizza goes positively classy here with grilled vegetables, pesto and red onions.

Per serving: about
- 420 calories
- 21 g fat
- high source of fiber
- good source of iron
- 15 g protein
- 43 g carbohydrate
- excellent source of calcium

TIP: Pesto is readily available in the supermarket, but you can just as easily make your own. In food processor, chop 1 cup (250 mL) packed fresh basil, 1/2 cup (125 mL) freshly grated Parmesan cheese, 2 tbsp (25 mL) pine nuts, 1 large clove garlic and 1/2 tsp (2 mL) each salt and pepper. With motor running, gradually pour in 1/2 cup (125 mL) olive oil, puréeing until smooth. Makes about 1 cup (250 mL).

Mediterranean Pizza

3	plum tomatoes, thinly sliced (8 oz/250 g)	3
1/3 cup	chopped black olives	75 mL
1 tbsp	chopped fresh basil (or 1 tsp/5 mL dried)	15 mL
1/4 tsp	pepper	1 mL
2 tsp	olive oil	10 mL
1-1/2 cups	shredded Monterey Jack cheese (about 6 oz/175 g)	375 mL
	CRUST	
1/4 cup	cornmeal	50 mL
1-3/4 cups	all-purpose flour	425 mL
1 tbsp	baking powder	15 mL
1 tsp	salt	5 mL
1/3 cup	cold shortening	75 mL
3/4 cup	milk	175 mL

● CRUST: Sprinkle 15- x 10-inch (40 x 25 cm) rimmed baking sheet with 1 tsp (5 mL) of the cornmeal; set aside.

● In bowl, combine remaining cornmeal, flour, baking powder and salt; with pastry blender or two knives, cut in shortening until coarse crumbs form. Add milk all at once; stir with fork to make soft, slightly sticky dough. Turn out onto lightly floured surface; knead 10 times. Roll out to fit pan.

● Arrange tomatoes over crust; sprinkle with olives, basil and pepper. Drizzle with oil; sprinkle with cheese. Bake in bottom third of 425°F (220°C) oven for about 15 minutes or until cheese is bubbly and crust is browned. Let cool for 5 minutes before cutting. Makes 6 servings.

With no-cook toppings and a no-fail quick-bread crust, this family-size pizza is a snap to put together for weeknight suppers.

Per serving: about
- 405 calories
- 23 g fat
- good source of iron
- 13 g protein
- 36 g carbohydrate
- excellent source of calcium

Ever-Popular Pasta

Whether you're inviting friends over for a feast or fixing supper at the end of the day, you can always solve any menu dilemma with pasta. Versatile and quick to make, it's perfect with vegetables, mixes satisfyingly with beans and lentils — and definitely earns its keep in a kitchen.

Pasta e Fagioli ▶

Normally, *pasta e fagioli is a soup, but here it's a bowl of pasta embellished with red kidney beans and bright-green spinach that's tossed in just long enough for the leaves to wilt and soften.*

Per serving: about
- 555 calories
- 24 g protein
- 8 g fat
- 100 g carbohydrate
- very high source of fiber
- good source of iron

3 cups	orecchiette or shell pasta (about 8 oz/250 g)	750 mL
1	potato, peeled and diced	1
1 tbsp	olive oil	15 mL
4	cloves garlic, minced	4
1	large carrot, sliced	1
1	onion, chopped	1
1/4 tsp	each salt and pepper	1 mL
1	can (19 oz/540 mL) Italian-style stewed tomatoes	1
1	can (19 oz/540 mL) red kidney beans, drained and rinsed	1
4 cups	fresh spinach, trimmed and torn into bite-size pieces	1 L
1/4 cup	freshly grated Parmesan cheese	50 mL

● In large pot of boiling salted water, cook pasta and potato for 8 to 10 minutes or until tender but firm. Drain well and return to pot.

● Meanwhile, in saucepan, heat oil over medium heat; cook garlic, carrot, onion, salt and pepper, stirring occasionally, for about 8 minutes or until softened.

● Add tomatoes, breaking up with spoon; bring to boil. Stir in beans; heat through. Add to pasta mixture along with spinach; toss gently to coat. Serve sprinkled with Parmesan cheese. Makes 4 servings.

STOCKING YOUR KITCHEN FOR PASTA

Pasta is the perfect dish to serve as the fridge empties before the big shop. Here are some cupboard staples and refrigerator keepers that will solve those "what to serve tonight" dilemmas:

● tomato-based pasta sauces, including those with extra vegetables, herbs and cheese
● cans of tomatoes, tomato sauce and tomato paste
● cans of mushrooms
● cans of corn
● cans of beans, lentils and chick-peas
● bags of sun-dried tomatoes and dried mushrooms
● jars of olives, roasted peppers and artichokes
● evaporated milk
● dried herbs, especially basil, thyme and oregano
● onions and garlic.

Harvest Tortellini Toss ▲

*It's not hard to get your daily
quota of healthful vegetables
when your supper pasta is
tossed with four favorites —
corn, peppers, onions and
zuchini.*

Per serving: about
- 550 calories
- 15 g fat
- very high
  source of fiber
- good source
  of iron
- 28 g protein
- 77 g carbohydrate
- excellent source
  of calcium

1 tbsp	olive oil	15 mL
1	onion, chopped	1
2 cups	sliced mushrooms	500 mL
1 tbsp	all-purpose flour	15 mL
2	each small zucchini and sweet peppers, chopped	2
1 cup	corn kernels	250 mL
2	cloves garlic, minced	2
1 cup	2% evaporated milk	250 mL
1/2 tsp	pepper	2 mL
1/4 tsp	salt	1 mL
1	pkg (1lb/500 g) fresh or frozen cheese tortellini	1
1/2 cup	freshly grated Parmesan cheese	125 mL
1/4 cup	chopped fresh basil	50 mL

● In nonstick wok or large skillet, heat oil over high heat; cook onion and mushrooms, stirring often, for 5 minutes. Reduce heat to medium-high; stir in flour. Add zucchini, sweet peppers, corn and garlic; cook, stirring often, for 5 minutes.

● Make well in center of vegetable mixture; add evaporated milk, pepper and salt. Cook, stirring, for 5 minutes or until thickened.

● Meanwhile, in large pot of boiling salted water, cook tortellini according to package directions. Drain and add to vegetable mixture along with half of the Parmesan and the basil; toss to combine. Serve sprinkled with remaining Parmesan. Makes 4 servings.

Tortellini with Mushrooms and Broccoli

2 tsp	olive oil	10 mL
2	cloves garlic, minced	2
1	onion, chopped	1
3 cups	sliced mushrooms (8 oz/250 g)	750 mL
1/2 tsp	dried basil	2 mL
1/4 tsp	each salt and pepper	1 mL
1/2 cup	vegetable stock	125 mL
1 tbsp	white wine vinegar	15 mL
1	pkg (1 lb/500 g) frozen cheese tortellini	1
3 cups	broccoli florets (about 8 oz/250 g)	750 mL
1/4 cup	freshly grated Parmesan cheese	50 ml

● In large nonstick skillet, heat oil over medium heat; cook garlic and onion, stirring occasionally, for 5 minutes or until softened.

● Add mushrooms, basil, salt and pepper; cook, stirring often, for about 10 minutes or until mushrooms are softened and moisture is evaporated. Remove from heat; stir in stock and vinegar.

● Meanwhile, in large pot of boiling salted water, cook tortellini for 7 minutes. Add broccoli; cook for about 3 minutes or until pasta is tender but firm and broccoli is tender-crisp. Drain and return to pot, reserving 1/3 cup (75 mL) cooking liquid.

● Add mushroom mixture; stir gently to combine, adding reserved cooking liquid to moisten, if desired. Top servings with cheese. Makes 4 servings.

Store-bought cheese-filled tortellini and ravioli take no more time to cook than plain pasta, and they offer extra nutritional value. Include the broccoli with the pasta in the same pot and save on cleanup.

Per serving: about
- 445 calories
- 12 g fat
- high source of fiber
- good source of iron
- 22 g protein
- 63 g carbohydrate
- excellent source of calcium

One-Pot Macaroni and Cheddar

2 cups	macaroni (8 oz/250 g)	500 mL
1-1/2 cups	thinly sliced carrots	375 mL
2 cups	milk	500 mL
2 tbsp	all-purpose flour	25 mL
1 tbsp	Dijon mustard	15 mL
2 tbsp	butter	25 mL
2 cups	shredded Cheddar cheese (8 oz/250 g)	500 mL
4	green onions, chopped	4
1/4 tsp	each salt and pepper	1 mL

● In large pot of boiling salted water, cook macaroni for 5 minutes. Add carrots; cook for 4 to 5 minutes or until pasta and carrots are tender but firm. Drain in colander; set aside.

● In same saucepan, whisk together milk, flour and mustard; cook over medium-high heat, whisking, for 2 to 3 minutes or until thickened and smooth. Reduce heat to medium; cook for 1 minute longer.

● Stir in pasta mixture and butter; cook, stirring, for 2 to 3 minutes or until heated through. Stir in cheese and onions; cook for 1 minute or until cheese melts. Season with salt and pepper. Makes 4 servings.

This quick-to-make meal will really satisfy. Serve with crisp celery sticks and radishes.

Per serving: about
- 580 calories
- 28 g fat
- excellent source of calcium
- 26 g protein
- 55 g carbohydrate

Vegetable and Penne Toss

Light cream cheese smooths out a mixed vegetable sauce and clings delectably to the penne.

Per serving: about
- 610 calories
- 16 g fat
- very high source of fiber
- 19 g protein
- 99 g carbohydrate
- good source of iron

4	tomatoes	4
2	zucchini	2
2 tbsp	olive oil	25 mL
2 cups	button mushrooms, halved	500 mL
3	cloves garlic, minced	3
1	onion, chopped	1
1 tbsp	dried basil	15 mL
1 tsp	each dried oregano and salt	5 mL
1/2 tsp	pepper	2 mL
Pinch	crushed hot pepper flakes	Pinch
1 tbsp	red wine vinegar	15 mL
4 oz	light cream cheese, softened	125 g
5 cups	penne (or other short pasta), about 1 lb (500 g)	1.25 L

● Chop 3 of the tomatoes; cut remaining tomato into thin wedges. Quarter zucchini lengthwise; cut crosswise into slices. Set aside.

● In skillet, heat oil over medium heat; cook mushrooms, garlic, onion, basil, oregano, salt, pepper and hot pepper flakes, stirring often, for 4 minutes or until onion is softened.

● Stir in chopped tomatoes; increase heat to medium-high. Cook, stirring occasionally, for 5 minutes or until tomato juices are released.

● Stir in zucchini and vinegar; reduce heat to medium. Cook, stirring often, for 5 minutes or until zucchini is tender. Add cream cheese, stirring until blended.

● Meanwhile, in large pot of boiling salted water, cook penne for 8 to 10 minutes or until tender but firm; drain and return to pot. Add sauce and toss to coat. Serve garnished with tomato wedges. Makes 4 servings.

Three-Cheese Baked Penne

Roasted vegetables offer yet another imaginative variation on everyone's favorite comfort pasta — macaroni and cheese. It's especially easy on the cook, too, because the casserole can wait for a day in the fridge before baking.

Per serving: about
- 675 calories
- 33 g fat
- very high source of fiber
- good source of iron
- 29 g protein
- 68 g carbohydrate
- excellent source of calcium

1	each sweet red and yellow pepper, chopped	1
8 oz	mushrooms, quartered	250 g
2	zucchini, diced	2
1	small eggplant, diced	1
3	cloves garlic, minced	3
1/4 cup	olive oil	50 mL
1/2 cup	chopped fresh parsley	125 mL
2 tbsp	chopped fresh basil (or 2 tsp/10 mL dried)	25 mL
1/2 tsp	dried rosemary	2 mL
Pinch	each salt and pepper	Pinch
5 cups	penne pasta (1 lb/500 g)	1.25 L
1	can (28 oz/796 mL) spaghetti sauce	1
8 oz	mozzarella cheese, shredded	250 g
8 oz	fontina cheese, diced	250 g
1 cup	freshly grated Parmesan cheese	250 mL

● In bowl, toss together red and yellow peppers, mushrooms, zucchini, eggplant, garlic and oil; spread on rimmed baking sheet. Bake in 500°F (260°C) oven, stirring twice, for 20 minutes or until softened. Transfer to greased 13- x 9-inch (3 L) baking dish. Toss with 1/3 cup (75 mL) of the parsley, basil, rosemary, salt and pepper.

● Meanwhile, in large pot of boiling salted water, cook penne for 8 to 10 minutes or until tender but firm. Drain well; rinse under cold water.

● Add to baking dish with spaghetti sauce, mozzarella, fontina and half of the Parmesan cheese; toss to combine. Sprinkle with remaining Parmesan and parsley. *(Can be prepared to this point, covered and refrigerated for up to 1 day.)* Bake in 375°F (190°C) oven for 35 to 40 minutes or until bubbly. Makes 8 servings.

Fall Vegetables and Fusilli

3 cups	fusilli pasta (about 8 oz/250 g)	750 mL
1/4 cup	butter	50 mL
1-1/2 cups	diced carrots	375 mL
1 cup	chopped celery	250 mL
1 cup	chopped onions	250 mL
4	cloves garlic, minced	4
2 cups	quartered mushrooms	500 mL
2 cups	cubed zucchini	500 mL
1	large sweet red pepper, diced	1
1/4 cup	all-purpose flour	50 mL
2 tsp	dry mustard	10 mL
2 tsp	dried thyme or basil	10 mL
1-1/2 tsp	salt	7 mL
1/2 tsp	pepper	2 mL
2 cups	milk	500 mL
1-1/2 cups	vegetable stock	375 mL
1	can (19 oz/540 mL) chick-peas, drained	1
2 cups	shredded Cheddar cheese (8 oz/250 g)	500 mL
1-1/2 cups	fresh bread crumbs	375 mL
1/2 cup	minced fresh parsley	125 mL

● In large pot of boiling salted water, cook fusilli for 8 to 10 minutes or until tender but firm. Drain and rinse under cold water; drain again and set aside.

● Meanwhile, in large heavy saucepan, melt butter over medium heat; cook carrots, celery, onions and garlic, stirring often, for 5 minutes. Add mushrooms, zucchini and red pepper; cook for about 5 minutes or until softened.

● Stir in flour, mustard, thyme, salt and pepper; cook for 2 minutes, stirring. Gradually stir in milk and stock; bring to simmer and cook, stirring, for 5 minutes or until thickened. Add chick-peas and fusilli. Transfer to 13- x 9-inch (3 L) baking dish. *(Recipe can be prepared to this point, covered and refrigerated for up to 1 day. Or freeze in airtight container for up to 2 months; thaw and add 10 minutes to baking time.)*

● Toss together cheese, bread crumbs and parsley; sprinkle over casserole. Bake in 375°F (190°C) oven for about 45 minutes or until crusty on top and bubbly. Makes 8 servings.

E*njoy our comfy pasta and chick-pea casserole for supper or lunch.*

Per serving: about
- 455 calories
- 19 g fat
- excellent source of calcium
- high source of fiber
- 19 g protein
- 53 g carbohydrate
- good source of iron

Creamy Tomato Shells

1 tbsp	vegetable oil	15 mL
2	cloves garlic, minced	2
1	onion, chopped	1
1 tbsp	dried basil	15 mL
1/2 tsp	pepper	2 mL
1/4 tsp	each salt and hot pepper sauce	1 mL
1	can (28 oz/796 mL) tomatoes	1
1 cup	2% evaporated milk	250 mL
5 cups	pasta shells	1.25 L
1/4 cup	freshly grated Parmesan cheese	50 mL

● In saucepan, heat oil over medium heat; cook garlic, onion, basil, pepper, salt and hot pepper sauce, stirring occasionally, for about 5 minutes or until softened.

● In blender or food processor, purée tomatoes; add to pan and bring to boil. Reduce heat and boil gently, stirring often, for about 20 minutes or until thickened. Remove from heat; stir in milk.

● Meanwhile, in large pot of boiling salted water, cook pasta for 8 to 10 minutes or until tender but firm; drain well and return to pot. Add sauce and toss to coat. Serve sprinkled with Parmesan cheese. Makes 4 servings.

A*dd calcium to your weekday pasta dinner with a splash of vitamin-rich evaporated milk.*

Per serving: about
- 635 calories
- 9 g fat
- very high source of fiber
- 25 g protein
- 113 g carbohydrate
- excellent source of iron and calcium

Quick Pasta with Spinach

Cottage cheese moistens a medley of onions, fresh herbs, spinach and radiatore — and pares cooking time off this pasta dish, too, since there's no sauce to make.

Per serving: about
- 460 calories
- 17 g protein
- 12 g fat
- 70 g carbohydrate
- high source of fiber
- excellent source of iron

4 cups	radiatore pasta (12 oz/375 g)	1 L
3 tbsp	olive oil	50 mL
1	onion, chopped	1
2	cloves garlic, minced	2
1 tsp	each dried thyme and oregano	5 mL
1	pkg (10 oz/284 g) fresh spinach, chopped	1
1/4 cup	vegetable stock	50 mL
1 tsp	lemon juice	5 mL
1/2 tsp	each salt and pepper	2 mL
1/2 cup	light cottage cheese	125 mL

● In large pot of boiling salted water, cook pasta for 8 to 10 minutes or until tender but firm; drain well and return to pot.

● Meanwhile, in large skillet, heat 2 tbsp (25 mL) of the oil over medium heat; cook onion, garlic, thyme and oregano, stirring occasionally, for about 5 minutes or until onions are softened. Add to drained pasta along with remaining oil.

● Add spinach, stock, lemon juice, salt and pepper; toss to coat well. Cook over low heat for about 4 minutes or until spinach is wilted. Stir in cottage cheese. Makes 4 servings.

Linguine with Tomatoes, Cheese and Jalapeños

Hot peppers add a kick to a fresh tomato-and-pasta toss.

Per serving: about
- 425 calories
- 18 g protein
- 11 g fat
- 63 g carbohydrate
- high source of fiber
- good source of calcium and iron

1 lb	linguine	500 g
2 tbsp	olive oil	25 mL
1 cup	finely chopped fresh parsley	250 mL
2 tbsp	minced pickled jalapeño pepper	25 mL
4	cloves garlic, minced	4
3	large tomatoes, chopped	3
1 cup	freshly grated Parmesan cheese	250 mL

● In large pot of boiling salted water, cook linguine for 8 to 10 minutes or until tender but firm; drain well and return to pot.

● Meanwhile, in nonstick skillet, heat oil over high heat; cook parsley, jalapeño pepper, garlic and tomatoes, stirring, for 1 minute. Add to linguine; toss to coat. Add Parmesan cheese; toss again. Makes 6 servings.

BASIC VEGETABLE STOCK

A recipe for a good basic stock is a must in every kitchen.

● In stockpot, heat 1 tsp (5 mL) vegetable oil over medium heat. Cook 2 carrots, 2 onions, coarsely chopped, plus 1 leek, coarsely chopped (white and light-green part only), and 1 stalk celery with leaves, chopped, stirring often, for 10 minutes or until softened but not colored. Add 10 stems fresh parsley, 3 sprigs fresh thyme (or 1/2 tsp/2mL dried), 10 peppercorns cracked, 2 bay leaves and 8 cups cold water and bring to a boil. Skim off foam. Reduce heat to medium and simmer, uncovered, for 40 minutes. Strain through fine sieve, gently pressing vegetables to extract liquid. Stir in 1/2 tsp salt. Makes about 5 cups (1.25 L).

Radiatore with Squash and Currants ▲

1/4 cup	olive oil	50 mL
3	cloves garlic, minced	3
1	onion, chopped	1
1 tbsp	cider vinegar	15 mL
2 tsp	packed brown sugar	10 mL
1/3 cup	currants	75 mL
1/4 tsp	each salt and pepper	1 mL
5 cups	radiatore pasta (1 lb/500 g)	1.25 mL
3 cups	diced peeled squash (1 small butternut)	750 mL
2 tbsp	freshly grated Parmesan cheese	25 mL

● In skillet, heat oil over medium-low heat; add garlic, onion, vinegar and sugar. Cover and cook, stirring often, for about 10 minutes or until onions are softened. Stir in currants, salt and pepper.

● Meanwhile, in large pot of boiling salted water, cook pasta and squash for about 8 minutes or until pasta is tender but firm. Reserving 1/2 cup (125 mL) cooking water, drain pasta and return to pot. Add reserved cooking water and onion mixture; toss to coat well. Serve sprinkled with Parmesan cheese. Makes 4 servings.

Although you may not think of teaming squash with pasta, we guarantee you'll love the flavor combo once you try it. The currants add a touch of sweetness and contrast nicely with the splash of cider vinegar and the salty cheese.

Per serving: about
- 730 calories
- 17 g fat
- very high source of fiber
- 17 g protein
- 130 g carbohydrate
- good source of iron

TIP: Small pasta shapes are perfect for holding sauce. Instead of radiatore, you can use penne, fusilli, rotini or rotelle.

Grilled Polenta with Mushrooms ◄

1/3 cup	olive oil	75 mL
1/4 cup	balsamic or red wine vinegar	50 mL
1 tsp	Dijon mustard	5 mL
Pinch	each salt and pepper	Pinch
8	plum tomatoes, halved lengthwise	8
2	sweet yellow peppers, cut in eighths	2
4	portobello mushrooms, (about 12 oz/350 g), stemmed	4
1/4 cup	shredded fresh basil	50 mL
	POLENTA	
1 tsp	salt	5 mL
1 cup	cornmeal	250 mL
1/2 cup	freshly grated Parmesan cheese	125 mL

● POLENTA: In heavy saucepan, bring 4 cups (1 L) water and salt to boil; reduce heat to low. Gradually whisk in cornmeal; cook, stirring often with wooden spoon, for 20 to 25 minutes or until thick enough to mound on spoon. Stir in Parmesan cheese. Spread in greased 9-inch (2.5 L) cake pan, smoothing with spatula. Refrigerate for at least 2 hours or until firm. *(Polenta can be covered and refrigerated for up to 24 hours.)*

● In small saucepan, whisk together oil, vinegar, mustard, salt and pepper; brush 1/3 cup (75 mL) over tomatoes, yellow peppers and mushrooms.

● Place tomatoes, skin side down, on greased grill over medium-high heat; add yellow peppers and mushrooms, smooth side down. Close lid and cook, turning peppers and mushrooms once, for about 8 minutes or until mushrooms yield when gently pressed. Remove mushrooms; cut into 1/2-inch (1 cm) thick strips if desired. Keep warm. Meanwhile, cook remaining vegetables for 2 to 4 minutes longer or until softened and tender; add to mushrooms.

● Cut polenta into 4 squares; cut each diagonally in half. Place triangles on greased grill; close lid and cook, turning once, for 10 minutes or until crusty and grill-marked. Meanwhile, add saucepan of remaining vinegar mixture to grill; heat until steaming. Serve polenta topped with vegetables; drizzle with vinegar mixture. Sprinkle with basil. Makes 4 servings.

Enjoy hearty polenta a new way — cut into triangles, brushed with olive oil and grilled until crusty and marked. Add portobello mushrooms, either whole or sliced, tomatoes, basil and peppers for a supper that takes you off on a delectable taste trip to the Mediterranean.

Per serving: about
- 405 calories
- 23 g fat
- high source of fiber
- 11 g protein
- 41 g carbohydrate
- good source of calcium and iron

Penne with Garlic Pesto

2/3 cup	vegetable stock	150 mL
2	large cloves garlic	2
1 cup	packed fresh basil leaves	250 mL
1/3 cup	freshly grated Parmesan cheese	75 mL
2 tbsp	pine nuts	25 mL
4 cups	penne (12 oz/375 g)	1 L
2	large tomatoes, seeded and diced	2

● In small microwaveable dish or in saucepan, combine stock with garlic; microwave at High or simmer on stove top for about 5 minutes or until garlic is softened. Let cool.

● In food processor, finely chop basil; blend in stock mixture. Add Parmesan cheese and pine nuts; chop until nuts are fine. *(Pesto can be refrigerated in airtight container for up to 24 hours.)*

● In large pot of boiling salted water, cook penne for 8 to 10 minutes or until tender but firm; drain well and return to pot. Add tomatoes and pesto; toss to coat. Makes 4 servings.

Stock replaces the oil in this pasta dish that has a head-start garlic-and-basil pesto step.

Per serving: about
- 400 calories
- 7 g fat
- high source of fiber
- 17 g protein
- 68 g carbohydrate
- good source of iron

Roasted Red Pepper Lasagna

W*hile the red peppers
in the title might make you
think this many layered,
sky-high lasagna is a
summer-only recipe, keep in
mind that jarred roasted
sweet red peppers are both
affordable and available in
the off season.*

Per serving: about
- 555 calories
- 23 g fat
- very high
  source of fiber
- 24 g protein
- 67 g carbohydrate
- excellent source
  of calcium and iron

TIP: If using lasagna noodles
with ruffled edges, you will
need 21 noodles (about
3/4 lb/375 g).

8 oz	flat spinach lasagna noodles (about 12)	250 g
1	pkg (10 oz/284 g) fresh spinach, trimmed	1
	TOMATO SAUCE	
1 tbsp	olive oil	15 mL
1	onion, chopped	1
4	cloves garlic, minced	4
2	carrots, peeled and diced	2
3 cups	sliced mushrooms (8 oz/250 g)	750 mL
1-1/2 tsp	dried oregano	7 mL
1 tsp	dried thyme	5 mL
1/2 tsp	salt	2 mL
1/4 tsp	each pepper and hot pepper flakes	1 mL
2	cans (each 19 oz/540 mL) tomatoes, chopped	2
1	jar (313 mL) roasted red peppers, drained and chopped	1
1/4 cup	tomato paste	50 mL
2 tbsp	white wine vinegar	25 mL
	BÉCHAMEL SAUCE	
1/4 cup	butter	50 mL
1/2 cup	all-purpose flour	125 mL
4 cups	milk	1 L
1/2 tsp	salt	2 mL
1/4 tsp	each pepper and nutmeg	1 mL
1 cup	shredded Asiago cheese	250 mL
1/2 cup	freshly grated Parmesan cheese	125 mL

● TOMATO SAUCE: In large wide saucepan,
heat oil over medium heat; cook onion and
garlic, stirring often, for 3 minutes. Add
carrots, mushrooms, oregano, thyme, salt,
pepper and hot pepper flakes; cook, stirring
often, for about 8 minutes or until
mushrooms are soft and liquid is evaporated.

● Stir in tomatoes, red peppers, tomato paste
and vinegar; bring to boil. Reduce heat and
boil gently, stirring often, for 1 hour or until
reduced to 5 cups (1.25 L) and thick enough
to mound on spoon.

● Meanwhile, in large pot of boiling salted
water, cook noodles, in batches, for
8 minutes or just until tender. With tongs,
transfer to dish of cold water. Drain; arrange
in single layer between damp tea towels.

● Stir spinach into pasta water; cook for
1 minute. Drain in sieve, pressing out all
liquid; chop coarsely. Set aside.

● BÉCHAMEL SAUCE: In saucepan, melt
butter over medium heat; stir in flour and
cook, stirring, for 3 minutes. Gradually
whisk in milk, salt, pepper and nutmeg.
Cook, whisking often, for 10 to 15 minutes or
until thickened. Whisk in half of the Asiago
cheese and 1/3 cup (75 mL) of the Parmesan.

● Spread one-quarter of the tomato sauce in
11- x 7-inch (2 L) baking dish; top with layer
of noodles, trimming to fit. Repeat layering.
Spread with one-third of the béchamel
sauce; top with layer of noodles. Scatter
spinach on top; sprinkle with remaining
Asiago. Top with layer of noodles, one-
quarter of the tomato sauce, another layer of
noodles and one-third of the béchamel
sauce; repeat final layering once. Cover with
foil. *(Lasagna can be prepared to this point
and refrigerated for up to 24 hours; add
about 10 minutes to first baking time.)*

● Bake on baking sheet in 375°F (190°C)
oven for 30 minutes. Uncover and sprinkle
with remaining Parmesan; bake for
30 minutes or until bubbly and golden. Let
stand for 20 minutes. Makes 6 servings.

Squash and Caramelized Onion Lasagna

1/3 cup	butter	75 mL
4	large onions, sliced	4
1/2 cup	all-purpose flour	125 mL
4 cups	milk	1 L
1/2 cup	freshly grated Parmesan cheese	125 mL
1 tsp	salt	5 mL
1/2 tsp	each pepper and grated nutmeg	2 mL
9	lasagna noodles	9
3 cups	chopped broccoli	750 mL
	SQUASH FILLING	
1-1/3 cups	light ricotta cheese	325 mL
1-1/3 cups	squash purée	325 mL
1	egg	1
1	egg yolk	1
1/2 cup	fresh bread crumbs	125 mL
2 tbsp	freshly grated Parmesan cheese	25 mL
1/4 tsp	each salt and pepper	1 mL
Pinch	grated nutmeg	Pinch

● In skillet, melt 2 tbsp (25 mL) of the butter over medium-low heat; cook onions, stirring occasionally, for 35 to 45 minutes or until golden. Set aside.

● Meanwhile, in heavy saucepan, melt remaining butter over medium heat; stir in flour and cook, stirring, for 2 minutes. Gradually whisk in milk; bring to boil. Reduce heat to medium-low; cook, stirring, for 10 to 15 minutes or until thickened. Remove from heat; stir in 1/4 cup (50 mL) of the Parmesan cheese, salt, pepper and nutmeg.

● Meanwhile, in large pot of boiling salted water; cook noodles for 8 to 10 minutes or until almost tender. Reserving cooking liquid, remove noodles from pot; rinse in cold water. Arrange in single layer on damp tea towel.

● Return reserved cooking liquid to boil. Add broccoli; cook for about 2 minutes or until almost tender. Drain and refresh under cold water; drain again. Set aside.

● SQUASH FILLING: In food processor, pulse ricotta with squash purée until very smooth. Transfer to large bowl; stir in egg, egg yolk, bread crumbs, Parmesan cheese, salt, pepper and nutmeg until well blended. Set aside.

● Set aside 1 cup (250 mL) of the cheese sauce. Arrange 3 noodles in single layer in greased 13- x 9-inch (3 L) baking dish. Spread with half each of the squash filling, broccoli, onions and remaining cheese sauce. Repeat layers.

● Top with remaining noodles and reserved cheese sauce. Sprinkle with remaining Parmesan cheese. Bake in 375°F (190°C) oven for about 40 minutes or until light golden and bubbly. Let stand for 10 minutes before serving. Makes 8 to 10 servings.

TIP: You will need about 4 cups (1 L) squash cubes to yield 1-1/3 cups (325 mL) purée. Use hubbard, butternut or buttercup varieties.

Lasagna has seen so many variations over the years, but none more delectable than this one. It's just right for a friendly Saturday-night get-together.

Per each of 10 servings: about
- 335 calories
- 16 g protein
- 13 g fat
- 39 g carbohydrate
- excellent source of calcium

SQUASH PURÉE

Squash purée is great as a side dish or as an ingredient in quick loaves, soups or as an alternative to pumpkin in pies. Hubbard, buttercup, butternut, delicata and acorn squash are all ideal. Freeze purée in convenient batches.

● Plan on about 3 lb (1.5 kg) whole squash or about 12 cups (3 L) cubed to yield 4 cups (1 L) purée.

● Place squash halves, flesh side down, in roasting pan. Pour in enough water to come 1 inch (2.5 cm) up side of pan. Bake in 400°F (200°C) oven for 30 to 60 minutes or until tender. Scrape flesh from shell. (Or, for easy-to-peel varieties, peel, seed and cube; steam for 10 to 12 minutes or until tender.) Let cool. Purée in food processor. *(Purée can be frozen in batches for up to 2 months.)*

Brunch Lasagna ◄

1 tsp	canola or vegetable oil	5 mL
3 cups	sliced mushrooms (8 oz/250 g)	750 mL
1	small onion, chopped	1
1	clove garlic, minced	1
1	sweet red or green pepper, chopped	1
2 tbsp	all-purpose flour	25 mL
1 tsp	dried basil or oregano	5 mL
1/2 tsp	each salt and pepper	2 mL
1-1/2 cups	1% milk	375 mL
2	pkg (each 10 oz/ 300 g) frozen broccoli, thawed	2
1/4 cup	chopped fresh parsley	50 mL
4	lasagna noodles	4
1	egg	1
1-1/2 cups	low-fat cottage cheese or ricotta cheese	375 mL
1 cup	shredded part-skim mozzarella cheese	250 mL
2 tbsp	freshly grated Parmesan cheese	25 mL
2 tbsp	fresh bread crumbs	25 mL

● In large nonstick skillet, heat oil over medium heat; cook mushrooms, onion, garlic and red pepper, stirring often, for about 5 minutes or until softened.

● Sprinkle with flour; stir to coat well. Stir in basil, salt and pepper. Gradually stir in 3/4 cup (175 mL) of the milk; cook, stirring often, for about 10 minutes or until sauce is smooth and thickened. Stir in broccoli and parsley; set aside. Cut lasagna noodles in half; set aside.

● In food processor or blender, blend together egg, cottage cheese and remaining milk until smooth. Spread one-third into lightly greased 8-inch (2 L) square glass baking dish. Spread with half of the broccoli mixture; cover with 4 noodle halves. Spread with half of the remaining cottage cheese mixture, then half of the mozzarella; cover with remaining noodles. Spread with remaining cottage cheese mixture, then mozzarella. Top with remaining broccoli mixture. Cover and refrigerate for at least 8 hours or for up to 16 hours.

● Combine Parmesan cheese with bread crumbs; sprinkle over broccoli mixture. Bake, uncovered, in 375°F (190°C) oven for about 40 minutes or until bubbling and crusty on top. Let stand for 10 minutes before serving. Makes 6 servings.

Here's a lightened-up dish you can put together the night before, then zip into the oven in the morning to keep any brunch effortless.

Per serving: about
- 275 calories
- 8 g fat
- high source of fiber
- 23 g protein
- 30 g carbohydrate
- excellent source of calcium

BUYING AND STORING TOFU

● Look for tofu in the fresh-vegetable section of a supermarket.
● Buy extra-firm or firm tofu for slicing or cubing. It has a meaty or cheeselike texture that works well in stir-fries, soups, kabobs and salads.
● Buy only fresh tofu. Always check the best-before date on the prepacked products. Tofu sold in an open tub should be very white, odorless and covered in a clear liquid.
● If possible, choose tofu that contains a calcium compound — for example, calcium sulphate or calcium chloride — to benefit from the extra calcium.
● Buy soft or silken tofu for mashing or for use in sauces, dips and dressings.
● Store in the refrigerator for up to a week, changing the water weekly.

Perogies for a Crowd

Perogy Dough

It only makes sense to prepare enough perogies to freeze or divvy up among family and friends. Invite everyone over to roll out the dough and fill the perogies together, before you share the feast.

8 cups	all-purpose flour	2 L
4 tsp	salt	20 mL
1-1/2 cups	milk	375 mL
1-1/3 cups	sour cream	325 mL
2	eggs	2

● In large bowl, stir flour with salt. Whisk together milk, sour cream and eggs; stir into dry ingredients just until soft shaggy dough forms.

● Turn out onto lightly floured surface; knead for 1 minute or until smooth. Divide into quarters; wrap each in plastic wrap and let rest for 20 minutes. Makes enough for 7-1/2 dozen perogies.

Potato and Roasted Garlic Filling

Per serving with Potato and Roasted Garlic Filling: about
- 530 calories
- 15 g fat
- high source of fiber
- 14 g protein
- 83 g carbohydrate
- excellent source of iron

2-1/2 lb	potatoes, peeled and quartered	1.25 kg
1 tbsp	vegetable oil	15 mL
10	cloves garlic, quartered	10
1/2 cup	milk	125 mL
1/3 cup	cream cheese, softened	75 mL
3/4 tsp	each salt and pepper	4 mL

● In large pot of boiling salted water, cover and cook potatoes for about 20 minutes or until tender. Drain well and return to pot; mash with potato masher until smooth.

● Meanwhile, in small saucepan, heat oil over medium-high heat. Add garlic and reduce heat to medium-low; cook, stirring occasionally, for 8 to 10 minutes or until golden and softened. Mash garlic and add to mashed potatoes along with milk, cream cheese, salt and pepper; stir just until smooth. Let cool to room temperature. *(Filling can be refrigerated in airtight container for up to 24 hours.)* Makes 4 cups (1 L), enough for 7-1/2 dozen perogies.

Cheddar and Mushroom Filling

Per serving with Cheddar and Mushroom Filling: about
- 535 calories
- 18 g fat
- high source of fiber
- excellent source of iron
- 16 g protein
- 76 g carbohydrate
- good source of calcium

2 tbsp	butter	25 mL
7 cups	chopped mushrooms (about 1-1/4 lb/625 g)	1.75 L
5	onions, chopped	5
1/2 tsp	each salt and pepper	2 mL
2 tbsp	cider or white wine vinegar	25 mL
2 cups	shredded old Cheddar cheese (about 5 oz/150 g)	500 mL

● In large heavy saucepan, melt butter over medium-high heat; cook mushrooms, onions, salt and pepper, stirring often, for 5 minutes. Reduce heat to medium; cook, stirring often, for 30 minutes or until mushrooms are softened and most of the liquid is evaporated.

● Stir in vinegar; cook for 3 minutes. Let cool for 5 minutes. Stir in cheese. Let cool. *(Filling can be refrigerated in airtight container for up to 24 hours; stir well before using.)* Makes 4 cups (1 L), enough for 7-1/2 dozen perogies.

TO ASSEMBLE PEROGIES

1	batch Perogy Dough (recipe, p. 88)	1
1	batch Potato and Roasted Garlic Filling or Cheddar and Mushroom Filling (recipes, p. 88)	1

● On lightly floured surface, roll out one of the quarters of dough at a time into 17-inch (43 cm) circle. With dry pastry brush, brush any excess flour off dough. Using 3-inch (8 cm) round cutter, cut dough into circles.

● Place rounded 1 tsp (5 mL) filling in center of one half of each circle. With different pastry brush, brush edges lightly with water. Fold dough over filling to form semicircle; pinch edges together firmly to seal. If desired, crimp by hand or with perogy crimper. Place on dish towel-lined baking sheet. *(Perogies can be prepared to this point, arranged in 2 layers between waxed paper in airtight container and refrigerated for up to 24 hours; or freeze in single layer, then store in airtight containers for up to 3 weeks.)* Makes about 7-1/2 dozen perogies.

TIP: To make triangular perogies, roll each quarter of dough into 14- x 10-inch (35 x 25 cm) rectangle. Cut lengthwise into 4 strips; cut each strip crosswise into seven 2-inch (5 cm) pieces. Fill each with 1 tsp (5 mL) filling; fold diagonally to form triangle. Makes about 9 dozen perogies.

Perogy Feast ▼

Half	batch perogies (recipe above)	Half
3 tbsp	butter	50 mL
1	large onion, thinly sliced	1
	Sour cream (optional)	

● In large pot of boiling salted water, cook perogies, in batches and stirring gently to prevent sticking, for 3 to 4 minutes for fresh, or 5 to 6 minutes for frozen, on until perogies float to top. With slotted spoon, transfer to colander to drain.

● Meanwhile, in large heavy skillet, melt butter over medium heat; cook onion, stirring occasionally, for 5 minutes or until golden.

● In batches, add perogies to skillet and cook, tossing to coat, for about 3 minutes or until lightly golden and heated through. Serve with sour cream (if using). Makes 6 servings.

TIP: For a whole batch, increase onion to 3 and butter to 1/3 cup (75 mL). Layer perogies in roasting pan; bake in 370°F (190°C) oven for 20 minutes, stirring or tossing halfway through.

The Contributors

Photography Credits

FRED BIRD:
pages 23, 45, 49.

DOUGLAS BRADSHAW:
pages 11, 41, 63, 65, 71, 84.

PETER CHOU:
pages 24, 50, 75.

PAT LACROIX:
page 20.

VINCENT NOGUCHI:
pages 15, 39, 58.

PAUL ORENSTEIN:
page 12.

CURTIS TRENT: page 88,
and photo of Elizabeth Baird
and Test Kitchen staff.

MICHAEL VISSER: page 4.

MICHAEL WARING: pages
16, 36, 57, 70, 76.

ROBERT WIGINGTON: front
cover, and pages 6, 8, 19, 29,
33, 35, 53, 61, 66, 72, 81, 86.

In the Canadian Living *Test Kitchen. From left: Kate Gammal, Susan Van Hezewijk, Donna Bartolini (Test Kitchen manager), Jennifer MacKenzie, Daphna Rabinovitch (associate food director) and Elizabeth Baird (food director). Absent from photo: Heather Howe and Emily Richards.*

Special Thanks

The year 1997 marks a decade of *Canadian Living* cookbooks, the result of a *Canadian Living* partnership with Random House of Canada and Madison Press. Many people have contributed to the success of our hardcover and paperback collections. Notable at Random House are president and publisher David Kent; mass marketing sales manager (Ballantine Books) Duncan Shields; vice-president of sales/marketing Kathy Bain; sales manager (trade) Lorraine Symmes; marketing manager Pat Cairns; publicity manager (international division) Sheila Kay; and senior publicist Cathy Paine. At Madison Press, under the leadership of president Albert E. Cummings and editorial director Hugh Brewster, its associate editorial director, the amazingly wonderful Wanda Nowakowska, who gets kudos for heading *Canadian Living* projects, with help from freelance editor Beverley Sotolov.

At *Canadian Living,* Robert Murray and Carol Ferguson pioneered *Canadian Living*'s cookbook program. Today, it flourishes with the guidance of publisher Caren King and editor-in-chief Bonnie Baker Cowan. Our Tested Till Perfect recipes are a team effort from associate food director Daphna Rabinovitch; the Test Kitchen, which under manager Donna Bartolini

includes Heather Howe, Jennifer MacKenzie, Susan Van Hezewijk and Emily Richards; and our valued food writers (see page 90 for their names and contributions). Vital to the Best series is the senior editor and organizer par excellence Beverley Renahan. I appreciate the excellence of senior editor Julia Armstrong, Michael Killingworth's copy department, managing editor Susan Antonacci and Info Access's Sharon Joliat and Barbara Selley. Thanks also to Tina Gaudino and Olga Goncalves, for their all-important behind-the-scenes work.

As for the visuals, the efforts of the *Canadian Living* art department under Cate Cochran; book designers Gordon Sibley and Dale Vokey; our talented photographers (see above for their names), who are aided in their creativity by food stylists Kate Bush, Ruth Gangbar, Jennifer McLagan, Olga Truchan, Lucie Richard and Claire Stancer, and props stylists Susan Doherty-Hannaford, Maggi Jones, Patti LaCroix, Bridget Sargeant, Shelly Tauber and Janet Walkinshaw, are all essential to *Canadian Living* and to the Best series.

My sincere thanks to one and all.

Elizabeth Baird

Index

Over 100 scrumptious vegetarian recipes!

Look to CANADIAN LIVING for all of the BEST!

Watch for more new books in the months ahead...
from Canadian Living so you know they're —THE BEST!